The Price Guide to
19th and 20th Century
BRITISH POTTERY

including Staffordshire Figures and Commemorative Wares

David Battie and Michael Turner

Antique Collectors' Club

British Library CIP Data
Battie, David
    Price guide to 19th and 20th century British pottery.
    1. Pottery, British — Collectors and collecting
    I. Title II. Turner, Michael
    III. Antique Collectors' Club
    738.8′0941   NK4085

    ISBN 0 902028 80 4

Published for the Antique Collectors' Club
by the Antique Collectors' Club Ltd.

Printed in England by
Baron Publishing, Woodbridge, Suffolk

*Frontispiece: a rare Staffordshire group commemorating The New Marriage Act of
1823. 7ins:17.8cm. £150 — £180.*

To Henrietta Victoria

Why not join —

The Antique Collectors' Club

The Antique Collectors' Club was formed in 1966 and now has a five figure membership spread throughout the world. It publishes the only independently run monthly antiques magazine *Antique Collecting* which caters for those collectors who are interested in increasing their knowledge of antiques, both by increasing the members' knowledge of quality and discussing the factors which influence the price that is likely to be asked. The Antique Collectors' Club pioneered the provision of information on prices for collectors and still leads in the provision of detailed articles on a variety of subjects. There are specialist articles on most collecting subjects but there is nearly always an article on ceramics, David Battie and Michael Turner being regular contributors.

It was in response to the enormous demand for information on "what to pay" that the price guide series was introduced in 1968 with the first edition of *The Price Guide to Antique Furniture,* a book which broke new ground by illustrating the more common types of antique furniture, the sort that collectors could buy in shops and at auctions, rather than the rare museum pieces which had previously been used (and still to a large extent are used) to make up the limited amount of illustrations in books published by commercial publishers. Many other price guides have followed, all copiously illustrated, and greatly appreciated by collectors for the valuable information they contain, quite apart from prices.

Club membership, which is open to all collectors, costs £7.95 per annum. Members receive free of charge *Antique Collecting,* the Club's magazine (published every month except August), which contains well-illustrated articles dealing with the practical aspects of collecting not normally dealt with by magazines. Prices, features of value, investment potential, fakes and forgeries are all given prominence in the magazine.

Among other facilities available through the Club are private buying and selling facilities, the longest list of "For Sales" of any antiques magazine, an annual ceramics conference and the opportunity to meet other collectors at your local antique collectors' club. There are nearly eighty in Britain and so far a dozen overseas.

As its motto implies, the Club is an amateur organisation designed to help collectors to get the most out of their hobby: it is informal and friendly and gives enormous enjoyment to all concerned.

For Collectors   —   By Collectors   —   About Collecting

The Antique Collectors' Club, 5 Church Street, Woodbridge, Suffolk

Contents

Acknowledgements

Our thanks are due to all the experts at Sotheby's in Bond Street, especially Paul Mack, and at Sotheby's Belgravia who have helped with checking and information. To John May, doubly, both for the information contained in his book and secondly for his reading the Commemorative section and for his helpful comments and criticism. To Geoffrey Godden on whose Encyclopaedia of Marks (see Bibliography) the factory dating was primarily based. To Paul Atterbury also thanks for reading and correcting, particularly on the Minton and Doulton pieces. We must thank all the collectors and dealers who have lent objects singling out Sarah Battie, Mr. and Mrs. W. Avery and Miss Lucy Thobboron. We are indebted to John and Diana Steel for their continuing patience and understanding in the extended preparation of this book and to Jeanette Kinch and the other photographers at Sotheby's for taking the photographs and to Mary Bowring and Caroline Fisher for sorting them. Lastly thanks to Sarah Battie for typing some of the copy, reading all of it, and for her helpful comments.

Introduction

This book, the companion to the *Price Guide to 19th and 20th Century British Porcelain,* uses the word pottery in the title to avoid making it any more unwieldy than it already is. It actually covers earthenware, stoneware, caneware, terracotta, creamware and so on; all clay bodies that are not covered by the porcelain book. It has proved even more difficult to sort this book into logical sections, convenient both for the established collector and for the novice, the former wanting, for example, all the Mason's Ironstone grouped together, the latter only knowing they have a jug and curious to know its value.

Vast quantities of anonymous, mass-produced earthenwares were produced in Staffordshire during the nineteenth century and sorting out the few easily identifiable factories would have meant numbers of small categories and an unwieldy portfolio of unidentified factories at the end comprising half the book. One thing was clear from the start — Wedgwood was a law unto itself and has been given its own section. To have followed the pattern of the last book and made the sections follow the form of the object, be it jug or plate, would have cut through two other well established patterns of collecting, namely Commemoratives Wares and Staffordshire Figures. These have therefore been retained, the former only for events of national or international importance contemporary with the event, the latter split into Staffordshire Portrait and Titled Figures, and Staffordshire Miscellaneous. In both of these sections some pieces are, in fact, porcelain. The major events taking place in the nineteenth century that were commemorated ceramically are listed in Appendix III to be found on p.239. The rest of the book follows the previous pattern with groupings by form or use. A check list of the named factories with their dates is given in Appendix II, and a separate index is provided.

We have tried to introduce as full a range as possible of objects in each section, using variation only to make a particular point. They have been chosen to reflect the strength of interest in the particular field, which has led to a weighty Wedgwood section, but few (I hope not too few) of the endless remnants of transfer-printed services still to be found in secondhand and antique shops. It would be easy to extend most sections into a book the size of this one.

The price range of the pottery objects given in this book is from 50p to £1,000, a lower range than in the companion porcelain guide. A further difference lies in the balance of the number of pieces that fall in the upper bracket above £500. Very, very few nineteenth century pottery pieces fall into this category and most of those are from the first twenty years of the century with the possible exception of some Wedgwood. The collecting of early nineteenth century wares, mainly jugs, animals and figures, is well established and is only a logical continuation of the eighteenth century productions as the new century did not affect the pottery stylistically. These buyers form one market. Others revolve round commemorative wares, Staffordshire portrait figures, Wedgwood, teapots, blue and white, the collectors of particular factories or a style such as the new movement towards majolica. These are neat little categories but unfortunately, or perhaps fortunately for a healthy market, they overlap. The teapot collector will find himself in competition with the Wedgwood, the majolica, the commemorative and the blue and white; the blue and white will bid against the Wedgwood, the commemorative and the teapot, and so on. Only the Staffordshire portrait figure collector has the field to himself. The collectors are often in touch with one another, visiting each other's collections and subscribing to specialist magazines or clubs. They have tended in the past to buy almost exclusively from specialist dealers and if they subscribed to the catalogues from the large auction houses their dealers bid for them on commission. There has been a great upheaval in recent years with the auctioneers tending to usurp the dealers' position, private collectors are now much more likely to leave a bid with the auctioneer or bid themselves.

The prices in this guide are based on what the piece should fetch in one of the major London salerooms. The prices for a similar piece in a country auction at the bottom end of the range, say £80, could be higher; above this level it is likely to fetch less. The prices in the London rooms are more likely to be consistent. But prices can be greatly increased in the sale of a prestigious collection (although the additional cost will be reflected in a higher price when the piece is resold, assuming the pedigree can be proved; the presence of a collection label is a great plus factor) by the appearance of a new reference book, particularly if it helps establish differences in rarity, or by a programme on television or an article in a journal making reference to the subject — just as share prices are affected by favourable press comment.

Dealers are as various as the sands of the sea, some specialise in say, Staffordshire figures and will have a clientele entirely of collectors, English or American. Another may be more general and will have some Wedgwood, some Staffordshire figures and so on. Another may specialise in "shipping goods", buying container loads to ship to the Continent or the U.S.A. Other dealers never go near an auction house, relying on private calls or being brought pieces by "runners" who have no shop themselves but make a living plying between one shop and another, or between shops and the auction houses.

The price charged by an antique shop will depend on what the dealer paid for the object and/or what he thinks he can get for it; one should expect to pay in the region of ten per cent to double the upper limit. The type of shop can have a dramatic effect on the price one has to pay. A specialist dealer can obviously count on a higher price than can a general dealer, and collectors will frequent the former rather than the latter. Nevertheless some of the best buys may be had by buying, for example, a piece of pottery from an extremely smart furniture shop which has a few pots scattered around for decoration, some of which may have been priced years before.

The normally stable market can be upset by a private person who simply wants the piece, and cares little what the price should be, or by the decorator who buys pieces with the opposite purpose in mind to the collector. He may buy a vase to convert to a lamp, a jardinière to a waste paper basket or carpet bowls to stand in a bowl on a pine dresser. He is unconcerned with any apparently well established pattern of prices and may well pay double the accepted rate for something secure in the knowledge that it will sell once it is put with his other stock which he has selected equally carefully.

There has been a rising market over the last five years and it seems not unlikely that a slump is in the offing; whether only a minor hiccup, as in 1973, or a period lasting several years only time will tell. A combination of factors, apparently far removed from the personal world of collecting has brought this about; primarily the fall of the Shah of Persia. This last reduced the amount of oil to the West, increased its price, and as Britain has its own supply, strengthened the pound. The Continental and American buyers, who previously found Britain a cheap place to shop, now fell away and the market for a wide range of works of art went quiet. The exception, at the time of going to press was the market in English works of art, maybe because the English were buying against threatening inflation, maybe because the Conservative government in power gave a feeling of security or perhaps because (with income tax cuts and the relaxing of dividend restraint) there really was more money around. Or maybe the oil gave the English a sense of security, or . . .and so on. All this simply proves (and the picture will surely have changed by the time you read this) that antiques are a commodity like any other — supply and demand, fashion, politics, international finance, insurance charges and inflation all play a part in dictating the price you pay for them. There seems to be some sort of cycle, lasting about five to six years, of a strong market followed by a depressed couple of years, and the brave punter buys during the slump. Perhaps the most extreme example is that of the Chinese market in 1974 when fifteenth and sixteenth century blue and white porcelain fell in price, and an early Ming dish went, say, from £22,000 to £10,000 and would now fetch £30,000.

The investor has not moved into the pottery field to any great extent, probably because to invest any worthwhile sum of money a very large number of objects would have to be bought. Neither he, nor the decorator, has such a field day with the pottery market as he does with the porcelain with the result that the prices are relatively stable with a satisfactory annual increase. It is unwise to buy solely for investment. Buy only what you really want and like and you will remain happy; try playing the market without experience and you could end up the miserable owner of an unsaleable "investment".

Damage

Pottery which is damaged does not have such a large mark down in value as does the comparable porcelain piece. This is presumably because pottery being a softer material is more likely to be damaged and because there is something strangely "honest" about a cracked earthenware jug which one can accept, whereas the same in porcelain would be a constant irritation. However, damaged pieces tend to have less of an investment value, whereas a really superb specimen will shoot up at a higher rate. Buyers should always check every piece before purchasing and if possible get a receipt from the dealer stating that the piece is not damaged. This should prevent him trying to palm off a well restored piece. When buying at auction check to see whether it is policy to state any damage or restoration in the catalogue. If it is stated against the lot in which you are interested all well and good, but if not *do not assume the piece is in good condition,* the cataloguer may well have missed the restoration and most rooms cover such a contingency by stating in their Conditions of Sale that they cannot accept responsibility for any mistakes. It is advisable to ask for a member of the department concerned to check the piece for you.

David Battie
September 1979

Important Notice

This book is a price guide and the estimates given reflect actual prices reached at a major London auction room, mainly within the last year. Prices fluctuate from sale to sale, on some objects or classes of object quite wildly. The prices given are for good examples in good condition unless otherwise stated. A damaged or tired example could range from the lower estimate to zero, whereas a really superb example might fetch double the upper limit. If the book is being used to decide how much to pay for a similar piece from a dealer, his profit must be added to the estimate given of between ten per cent and double the upper limit.

Price Revision List

1st February annually
(The first list will be published in 1981)

The usefulness of a book containing prices rapidly diminishes as market values change, for prices can fall as well as rise.

In order to keep the prices in this book fully up-dated a revised price list will be issued on 1st February each year. This list will contain the current values of all the pieces illustrated in the book.

To ensure that you receive the Price Revision List yearly, complete a banker's order form and send it to the Antique Collectors' Club now.

The Price Revision List cost £1.60 a year by banker's order or £1.75 cash, from:—

THE ANTIQUE COLLECTORS' CLUB
5 CHURCH STREET, WOODBRIDGE
SUFFOLK

Bowls, Jardinières

Strictly speaking a jardinière is a container in which plants are grown and to perform this function must have a hole in the base, most coming with a stand to catch the water seepage. A similar object without the hole and usually more bucket-shaped is probably a cache-pot, used to disguise a common flower pot. No doubt some were made for dual purposes and are now made to fulfil even more functions such as umbrella holders, waste paper baskets or simply as decoration. Those made to stand on a tall matching column are particularly expensive, as they overcome the main drawback of all the bowl family — that of being difficult to view from the normal standing position. As most decoration is found on the sides, the most satisfactory viewpoint is at eye level, severely restricting their use.

Most jardinières were made for orangeries, terraces and conservatories and have usually suffered at the hands of careless gardeners and are chipped or cracked, high moulded reliefs on a soft earthenware body obviously being the most prone. Many come minus their stands.

Cache-pots are more likely to be chipped on the rim or cracked where a pot has been dropped in. Cracks, particularly, affect the value — thirty per cent to fifty per cent for even a small one. This section includes bowls made for wash stands which have become separated from the rest of the equipment (sets will be found in the Miscellaneous section) and which are now coming back into favour as receptacles for punch.

Josiah Spode c.1820
Diameter 12½ins:31.8cm. Printed mark
A toilet or washing bowl transfer printed in blue inside and out with the Italian pattern. Of typical rounded form and unmistakably a bowl from a washing set and, as such, somewhat undesirable but coming into favour for salads and punch. Complete with jug, £70 — £90.
£50 — £60

Charles James Mason & Co. c.1840
Diameter 13ins:33cm
A blue transfer printed barber's bowl, the centre with soldiers dressed in uniform of the 1790-1800 period. Barbers' bowls had gone out of fashion by the beginning of the 19th century and it is somewhat puzzling to find this throw-back, conceivably it was made to special order, possibly by the military. The print has been crudely adapted to fit the bowl from a larger dish, compare the border and figures with the meat dish on p.125. This example cracked and chipped; in good order, £40 — £60.
£20 — £30

Deakin and Son c.1840
Diameter 9½ins:24.5cm. Printed name
An earthenware bowl printed in green with blobbed enamel roughly following the print. Crude but effective and inexpensive, particularly so when one considers that it is a marked piece from an uncommon factory and easily datable.
£20 — £30

Clyde Pottery Co. mid-19th century
Diameter 10ins:25.2cm
Printed Clyde Pottery and title
An earthenware bowl transfer printed in black with Robert Burns' characters Tam O'Shanter and Souter Johnny, another print on the interior. Burns' character prints are common and the crude manufacture of this bowl does not make it of much interest to a collector.
£30 — £50

A Mason's ironstone bowl with a hand coloured black transfer print, 1813-25. 12⅜ins:31.4cm. Printed name. £60 — £80.

A pair of Minton majolica cache-pots. 16ins:40.7cm. Impressed Minton and date code for 1865. £400 — £600.

Minton 1858
Height 10ins:24.5cm. Impressed Minton and date code
A majolica jardinière and stand, glazed yellow and brown and tied with a blue ribbon. Not particularly brilliant, but an ideal interior decorator's piece and early of its type. Pair £380 — £450.
£180 — £200

William Brownfield c.1860
Height 37ins:94cm
A massive jardinière and stand modelled by H. Carriere-Belleuse and painted by Joseph Evans, unfortunately badly damaged. An exhibition piece of a type made by many of the larger factories in the second half of the century and which have generally vanished into museums or been destroyed. Had this been perfect, it would probably fetch in the region of £800 — £1,200.
£200 — £300

Minton c.1865
Height 16ins:40.6cm. Impressed Minton
A jardinière and stand in typical bright majolica colouration but the large size lumpy flowers are unattractive and the whole design is not altogether happy. This was not Minton's opinion as they exhibited at the 1851 International Exhibition. This example with cracked stand £40 — £60. Pair with stands in good condition £250 — £300.

£80 — £100

Minton 1870
Height 8ins:20.2cm
Impressed Minton and date code

An attractive majolica sweetmeat bowl coloured in blue, green, ochre and aubergine, the interior turquoise. Presumably one of a pair £150—£180. Not only a good piece for a majolica collector but also a good decorator's piece, ideal in a bathroom filled with soap or bath cubes.

£40 — £60

Royal Worcester 1870s
Height 8½ins:21.5cm. Impressed circle mark

An unusual earthenware bowl, the interior turquoise the exterior white tinged with purple, and looking suspiciously like Belleek porcelain. The supporting dolphins are green. It was a curious decision to mould this bowl in pottery as the spiky shell serration on the rim could hardly survive intact long.

£40 — £60

George Jones 1870s
Height 8ins:20.3cm. No mark

An attractively restrained Egyptionesque jardinière supported by sphinxes, the deep blue ground bordered in green and yellow.

£70 — £100

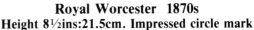

Minton c.1870
Height 17¾ins:45cm. Impressed name
A large and impressive majolica jardinière, the malachite-green earthenware body borded by lighter coloured reliefs. A well modelled and decorative object but its large size counts against it fetching a very high price.

£180 — £250

Minton 1870
Height 17½ins:44.5cm
Impressed name and date code
A large and well produced jardinière under brilliant coloured glazes, the interior, as usual, turquoise. In 1974 this piece fetched £80, but it seems likely that the very fine examples of majolica decoration could still rise fast over the next few years as interest grows.
£250 — £350

Royal Worcester c.1875
Height 7¼ins:18.4cm. Impressed crowned circle
A pair of turquoise-glazed basket weave cache-pots with purple handles and gilt details. Very much decorators' pieces; they would not interest a Worcester collector whose interest lies in the later finely painted porcelain.
£80 — £120

George Jones & Sons 1876
Height:19½ins:49.5cm
Impressed monogram, registration of design

A large jardinière well moulded and brightly coloured with flowers and birds in relief on a bright blue ground. An object both decorative and useful. Price for this piece with a few leaves missing; good example, £170 — £220.

£150 — £180

Minton 1876
Height 23ins:58.4cm. Impressed name and date code

A large earthenware jardinière painted in black with scrolling lotus after a 15th century Chinese original, on a bright turquoise ground. The shape, too, has come from a Chinese bronze but has been Europeanised about the feet.

£150 — £200

George Jones & Sons c.1880
Height 11¾ins:29.8cm
Impressed crescent mark

A majolica cache-pot moulded with birds and water plants and brightly coloured, the interior, as is so often the case, turquoise. The colouring in this example less attractive than it might appear from the photograph. Really attractive example, £120 — £180; with stand, £180 — £220; pair, £300 — £350.

£100 — £150

Doulton & Co. 1883
Height 7ins:17.8cm. Impressed rosette

The slate-grey bodies of these silicon-ware cache-pots are applied in white and green with studs, the separately moulded pieces being attached by slip and then fired. Unusually dreary for Doulton but typical of a whole class of wares produced at this period from small vases at £2 — £3 a piece up to umbrella stands at £100.

£50 — £70

Left:

Doulton c.1895
Height 40¼ins:102.5cm
Impressed rosette and name

A stoneware jardinière and stand moulded and applied with rosettes and leaves in typical blue, mustard and rust. Not by one of the readily identifiable Lambeth artists but made more on a mass-produced basis. Nevertheless, although not quite in the Studio collectors' range, a good decorative and usable object. Bowl alone, £100 — £150; stand, £100 — £150.

£250 — £300

Right:

Watcombe Pottery Co. c.1900
Height 28ins:98cm
Impressed Watcombe, Torquay

An unusually good example from a minor West Country pottery whose products are generally of little value, the terracotta ground with cream fairies and art nouveau foliage.

£150 — £200

A Minton "Secessionist" majolica jardinière, 1902-14. 8½ins:21.5cm. Printed mark and registration number. £60 — £80.

A Sunderland plaque, possibly by Moore and Co., unusually well coloured, c.1840. 7¾ins. x 8½ins:19.5cm x 21.5cm. Blurred impressed mark. £25 — £35.

Commemorative Wares

The use of the ceramic medium for recording important events, whether personal or national, has a long history dating back at least to the use of clay tablets in Mesopatamia in the third Millenium. In the seventeenth century births, marriages and coronations were frequently commemorated on pottery plates, jugs or tankards. The potter can react faster than almost any other artisan to produce in large quantities appropriately decorated objects, and a single, simply painted mug celebrating a marriage with the names and date could be produced in a few days. In the nineteenth century, when engraved scenes became the vogue, the length of time needed to produce the first would be considerably longer but after that numbers could be made very rapidly.

It should be remembered that with the poor communications in the seventeenth, eighteenth and early nineteenth centuries news of a royal marriage might not reach outlying districts for weeks or even months so that the commemorative jug might not appear on the scene until long after the event.

As the industrial revolution brought better communications with the canals and railways, so the number of suitable events to be commemorated increased; literacy, too, improved and longer inscriptions appear.

The commemorative pottery collector has a vast field from which to choose and must limit his collection by choosing some suitable theme, be it railwayana, politics or royalty. This section therefore runs parallel with the Staffordshire portrait figure section and some collectors devoted to a theme such as royalty might well collect across the divide, possibly also adding contemporary prints and books on the subject. Commemorative pieces of a purely local or personal nature are found under the general headings.

Although some of the early nineteenth century transfer-printed pieces, such as the Caroline plate, p. 32, are extremely rare, and generally speaking the later the item the more common it is, there are some curious anomalies. For example the William and Adelaide mug on p.37, made for their Coronation, is a lot less rare than the mug for Victoria.

As interest in commemorative material grows, as it seems to be doing quite fast, the less common items are becoming very expensive and even the commonest Diamond Jubilee mug which was perhaps 50p three years ago will now be £5. To cater for this need the larger auction houses hold specialist sales and one London dealer sells nothing else. There are also several books on the subject (see Bibliography).

This section has been arranged in date order and only those items which were made soon after the event they commemorate have been included here. For example, the endless Nelson jugs made throughout the century are included under Jugs, with the exception of his centenary.

The factory that produced the piece is rarely of importance to the commemorative collector (only in the case of Wedgwood is this not so); indeed the vast bulk of the pieces are unmarked, but marked examples are rising as the collectors of rare factories influence the price.

Staffordshire 1804
Height 8½ins:24cm. No mark

An earthenware jug printed in sepia with an American eagle, dated 1804 and a quotation from Jefferson. Thomas Jefferson was first elected President in 1800 and was re-elected to a second term of office in 1804, receiving 162 votes in the Electoral College to his Federalist opponent's 14. The jug was presumably either issued for the campaign, or to celebrate Jefferson's victory at the polls.

£100 — £120

Staffordshire c.1805
Height 7¼ins:18.4cm. No mark

A jug with a blue print on a pearl-ware body commemorating the death of Admiral Nelson.

£100 — £150

Staffordshire c.1805
Height 6ins:15.2cm. No mark

A rare jug printed in puce with Britannia mourning at Nelson's tomb. The reverse inscribed with Britannia's address on the Death of Lord Nelson. Variations in the print occur with no variation in price.

£120 — £180

Joshua Heath 1809
Diameter 8ins:20.3cm. Impressed I.H.

A rare plate transfer printed in blue with a crown, wreath and hopeful message. Probably first issued in 1793 at the outbreak of war between Britain and France whereas this example may record his Golden Jubilee. The border style and potter's marks are the only guide to the correct dating. Earlier example £200 — £250. The plate has a standard border from a service and is an interpretation of a Chinese export. Plate without the commemorative centre £2 — £3.

£100 — £120

Liverpool 1809
Height 15¾ins:40cm. No mark

A very large creamware jug commemorating the Jubilee of George III in 1809/10. The various prints include Wellington, Royal Coats of Arms and Justice bat-printed in black. The spout of this piece replaced in metal. Good example £400 — £500. Despite its rarity its exceptional size counts against it fetching the price it deserves.

£280 — £350

Herculaneum 1809
Height 7½ins:19.1cm. No mark

A rare creamware jug made for the Golden Jubilee of George III, the print in lilac depicting 'History' and Brittania over a prison and a statue of George (still extant in Liverpool). The scroll under the print refers to the amnesty George gave to debtors and certain prisoners. The reverse bears a print of a sailing vessel.

£400 — £600

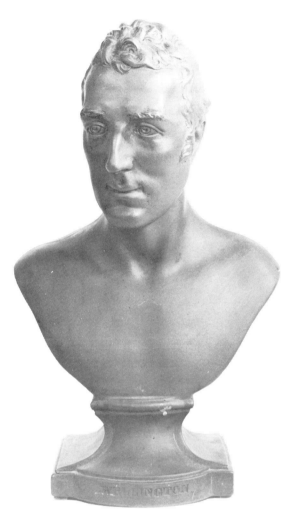

Staffordshire c.1812 (supposedly)
Height 4¾ins:12.1cm. No mark
A rare Earl Wellington jug moulded with a crudely coloured and titled portrait. Details in silver lustre. The date given is that which the jug should be, though this is doubtful as lustre only appeared in the first decade of the 19th century and, as with most innovations, reached the climax of quality in the first few years and then declined. Undoubtful example, £150 — £200.

£40 — £60

Spode and Copeland 1812-1816
Height 11½ins:29.1cm. Impressed title and names
A rare black basalt bust of the Duke of Wellington of youthful aspect. The factory was named Spode and Copeland only between 1797 and 1816 and since Arthur Wellesley was created Earl of Wellington in 1812, the bracket dates can be accurately determined. Basalt is, of course, a Wedgwood speciality but the fine quality of this piece indicates that Spode and Copeland were also well able to handle the material.
£150 — £200

Staffordshire 1812
Height 14ins:35.6cm. No mark
A large and rare jug with coloured transfer prints of scenes recording the defeat of Napoleon at Moscow, following the battle of Borodino on 7th September 1812. A similar print can be found on Derby porcelain jugs and variations occur on the pottery example with no noticeable variation in price.
£150 — £200

Swansea c.1810
Diameter 10¼ins:26cm. No mark

A rare pearlware bowl printed in bright blue with the busts of George III and Queen Charlotte, the exterior with a Chinese pattern. This print was first issued in 1793 at the outbreak of war with France; £300 — £400; but this example, lacking the anti-Jacobin slogans suggests the Golden Jubilee. This example cracked; good, £200 — £300.

£80 — £120

Staffordshire c.1815
Height 4½ins:11.4cm. No mark

A pearlware jug with a black transfer cartoon after Gillray, hand coloured, poking fun at the defeated Napoleon and probably made in April 1814 before going to Elba or after his imprisonment in July 1815 at Portsmouth before being sent to St. Helena.

£80 — £150

Sunderland 1816
Height 6ins:15.3cm. No mark

A moulded jug with a portrait of Princess Charlotte and her husband Prince Leopold, the details in pink lustre and bright enamels. Princess Charlotte was the daughter of the Prince Regent, the future George IV. She married Prince Leopold of Saxe-Coburg in 1816 but died in childbirth a year later.

£150 — £200

Sunderland c.1817
Height 5ins:12.8cm. No mark
A rare jug printed in black probably made to commemorate the death of Princess Charlotte in 1817.

£200 — £300

Staffordshire c.1816
Height 4½ins:11.8cm. No mark
Two views of a blue transfer printed mug with the mounted, named figures of the Duke of Wellington and Lord Hill. Well printed and produced not long after the end of the Napoleonic Wars. Lord Hill fought with Wellington at Waterloo and took over the defence of Paris in 1815; the same print can be found titled Lord Camberinere.
£120 — £180

A. Stevenson c.1820
Diameter 6¾ins:17.2cm
Impressed name above a star and ship

An exceptionally good plate with a brown printed portrait of Caroline made at the time of her trial. This example particularly unusual for being marked. Unmarked or less good prints from £120.

£200 — £250

Staffordshire c.1820
Height 3½ins:8.8cm. No mark

One of the rarest of all the Queen Caroline commemorative wares, this black print on an earthenware mug depicts honest John Bull weighing Caroline against George IV, who, despite being weighted with sacks of secrets and spies and the "green bag" used to carry documents at her trial, is heavily outweighed. For a full explanation of this fascinating intrigue see *Commemorative Pottery 1780-1900* by John and Jennifer May, London 1972.

£350 — £500

Possibly Swansea c.1820
4ins. x 2½ins:10.2cm x 6.4cm. No mark

A rare plaque naïvely moulded and coloured with a portrait of Queen Caroline, the unhappy consort of George IV. She returned to England from Italy in 1820 wearing the ostrich-feather hat in which she is usually depicted. The Tory leader under pressure from the King tried to pass a bill depriving her of her title, rights, prerogatives and immunities. The case was fabricated round her supposed adulteries but was withdrawn. When she tried to attend the Coronation in 1821 she was refused admission and died the following month.

£100 — £250

Staffordshire c.1820
Height 6½ins:16.4cm. No mark
An earthenware jug moulded with portraits of Queen
Caroline, lightly coloured and pink lustred, "Success
to Queen Caroline" impressed from type beneath the
bust. The enamels on this example flaking; in good
condition £120 — £150; well coloured £140 — £160.
£100 — £120

Staffordshire c.1822
Height 5¼ins:14cm. No mark
A rare earthenware jug commemorating the death of
Queen Caroline bearing a black transfer printed
portrait, the reverse with an inscribed plaque and
mourning figures. The neck has bands of pink and
gold lustre. This example with a good, clear print;
less well printed examples, from £100.
£150 — £250

Probably Scottish c.1822
7ins. x 8¾ins:17.8cm x 22.3cm. No mark
A rare plaque with a brightly coloured moulded
portrait of George IV. The ribbon at the base
impressed "Welcome George IV", and probably
commemorates his visit to Scotland in August 1822.
This example with extended firing cracks. Good
example, £180 — £250.
£100 — £150

Probably Lambeth c.1825
Height 8ins:20.3cm. No mark

A stoneware spirit flask as The Duke of York and titled. Unusually well detailed and glazed on the upper half an attractive honey brown, stopping smartly at his waist. The reverse impressed with a retailer's name and address. This is a good example of a rare flask; less well cast, £60 — £100.

£120 — £180

Staffordshire 1828
Height 5¼ins:13.3cm. No mark

A rare black-printed and copper lustre jug with the portrait of Daniel O'Connell who, although a Catholic and therefore banned from taking his seat in the Commons, stood for the County of Clare in the 1828 election. Despite fighting the popular Protestant holder Vesey Fitzgerald, he won the seat, this jug celebrating the event. Less crazed and worn or sharper printed example £180 — 250.

£100 — £140

Staffordshire c.1830
Diameter 6¾ins:17.2cm. No mark

A rare William and Adelaide plate made for the accession in 1830, not for the coronation the following year. The black print within a hectically moulded and eccentrically coloured border.

£200 — £300

Staffordshire 1830
Diameter 7½ins:19.1cm. No mark

A small plate, probably commemorating the accession of William IV and Adelaide, with their portraits and a crown on the rim and a scene in the centre. The somewhat smudgy colouration and the irrelevant scene do not make this amongst the most desirable of commemorative wares.

£25 — £35

Goodwin Bridgwood and Harris c.1830
Height 5½ins:13.9cm. Printed initials and lion

An uncommon jug made after the death of George IV, transfer printed in black with his portrait and the Royal arms. As the factory ran under this title from 1829-31 the date of the jug can be accurately determined. This example crazed; good specimen, £150 — £200.

£80 — £120

Staffordshire c.1831
Diameter 4¾ins:12.1cm. No mark

An uncommon plate probably made for the Coronation of William IV. The raspberry red print can also be found on a mug, £150 — £180. The moulded border is particularly unusual with cats, dogs, and a monkey trainer.

£120 — £150

*A Sunderland milk jug with a transfer of
Princess Charlotte, 1817. 5¾ins:14.5cm. £60 — £80.*

*A pearlware jug printed in puce with the portrait of
Sir Francis Burdett, M.P., who was arrested for
breach of privilege and imprisoned in the Tower,
c.1810. 5¼ins:13.2cm. £50 — £80.*

*A Staffordshire/Sunderland bowl printed in black and hand coloured with
a Crimean War print, c.1854. 11ins:28cm. £60 — £80.*

Staffordshire 1831
Height 8¼ins:20.9cm. No mark
A pair of well printed jugs with portraits of William IV and Adelaide to commemorate the Coronation. These jugs are not particularly rare but are well produced and decorative.
£150 — £250

Staffordshire 1831
Height 4ins:10.2cm. No mark
A mug transfer printed in lilac, with Adelaide on the reverse. The body slightly crazed; good example, £200 — £300.
£100 — £150

Staffordshire 1831
Height 8ins:20.3cm. No mark

A well printed (in lilac) and unusual William IV Coronation jug with scenes inside the Abbey. Coronation pieces of William IV are generally of a higher standard of design and production than those of Victoria and indeed than the majority of all commemorative wares of the first half of the 19th century.

£200 — £300

Staffordshire c.1832
Height 3¾ins:19.7cm. No mark

A Reform jug printed in black with the appropriate slogan, the reverse with a portrait of Earl Grey, who introduced the Reform Bill in 1831. The flowers include the National Emblems reinforcing the idea that Reform would be to the advantage of the British people.

£30 — £50

Staffordshire 1832
Height 4½ins:10.8cm. No mark

This black printed jug reflects the stirring up of interest in the most contentious issue of the time, the Reform Act of 1832, and has cartoons of the Whig and Tory leaders and William and Adelaide.

£120 — £180

Wedgwood c.1835
Height 5¾ins:14.6cm. Impressed Wedgwood pearl
Although Wedgwood, this jug is included in this section as its interest lies in its commemorative associations. The pearl ware body is printed in black with two political cartoons. Not, as one might think at first sight, connected with the Slavery Abolition Movement but an ironic comment on the joys of being British and the horrors of being foreign aimed at the French Freedom Movement.
£70 — £100

Probably Lambeth c.1836
Height 8ins:20.3cm. No mark
A stoneware spirit flask moulded with the dancing, singing figure of "Jim Crow", Thomas Dartmouth Rice as he really was. Rice was an American entertainer who came to England in 1836 and started the vogue for nigger minstrels.
£100 — £120

Possibly Fulham c.1838
Height 8½ins:21.6cm. No mark
A stoneware spirit flask made to commemorate the accession or Coronation of 1837/8. One side with a moulded portrait of Victoria, the reverse with her mother, the Duchess of Kent, their names impressed from type. A rare piece but modern copies are known, many in earthenware and this has slightly unsettled the market.
£70 — £100

Probably Sunderland c.1837
Height 5¾ins:14.6cm. No mark
A rare and attractive jug with a black transfer portrait of Queen Victoria, naïvely hand coloured. The background has a view of Windsor Castle and the reverse has the unconnected print of "The Sailor's Farewell", see p.83. The ground is well splashed pink lustre. Sunderland lustre can almost be dated by how good the definition of the lustre spots is, compare this with the pieces on pages 72 and 80. With handle and spout restored, £60 — £80.

£100 — £150

Staffordshire c.1838
Diameter 7ins:17.7cm.
No mark
An earthenware plate with flower-moulded border and transfer-printed with a portrait and inscription. The same print can be found on children's plates and other wares at similar prices.
£150 — £250

Probably Staffordshire 1838 and 1851
Diameter 6ins. and 6¾ins: 15.3cm and 17.2cm. No mark
These two earthenware plates photographed together show the loss of quality between the original 1838 Coronation issue and the 1851 production for the Great Exhibition.
£100 — £150 and £50 — £70

Probably Swansea 1838
Height 3¼ins:8.3cm. No mark
A rare mug made for the Coronation of 1838 with a lilac print of Queen Victoria and the dates of her birth, proclamation and Coronation. The same print but without the Coronation date and made for the accession is also known and is somewhat rarer, £550 — £650. Crazed or damaged examples down to £200.
£500 — £600

Staffordshire
c.1838
Height
9½ins:24.1cm.
No mark
An earthenware spirit flask in the form of Queen Victoria, the casting quite sharp under a rather "dead" brown glaze. More usually found in stoneware, £60 — £80, commemorative spirit flasks are being reproduced and collectors should be wary of earthenware examples (see Fakes section). This example, however, is apparently genuine.
£40 — £60

Staffordshire c.1840
Height 6¼ins:15.8cm. No mark

A pottery jug transfer printed in green with the portraits of Victoria and Albert and made to commemorate their marriage. The print can be found in other colours and the jug is a standard pattern with the addition of the special print.

£120 — £150

Staffordshire c.1840
Diameter 10¼ins:26cm. No mark

A simple plate commemorating the marriage of Victoria and Albert, the transfer print in blue. The triangle of black dots enclosing the print are caused by the spur, used to separate the stack of plates in the kiln which in this case has pierced the glaze allowing greasy matter to discolour the surrounding area.

£80 — £150

Staffordshire c.1840
Diameter 6¼ins:15.8cm. No mark

An attractive plate made for the marriage of Victoria and Albert. It can be found in several different colours including green and lilac with no great variation in price.

£120 — £150

Sunderland/Staffordshire c.1840
Height 6ins:15.2cm. No mark

A poorly moulded jug but a rare one, the reliefs of Queen Victoria and Prince Albert highly coloured on a copper lustre ground. A good example, if such exists, £60 — £80.

£45 — £60

Staffordshire/Sunderland c.1845
Height 8ins:21cm. No mark

A porcelain teapot transfer printed in puce and vaguely coloured with named figures of Albert and Victoria and the Princess Royal and the Prince of Wales, below lustre berries. The same print of the royal couple, but without the children was thought to have been produced at the time of their marriage, but this now seems unlikely. A service of teapot, jug, basin, twelve cups and saucers and two cake plates £100 — £150.

£30 — £40

Charles Meigh c.1850
Width 21½ins:54.5cm
Impressed opaque porcelain

A superb dish finely painted by Brammer for the 1851 Exhibition with Albert and Victoria greeting Sir Robert Peel at Windsor Castle. Earthenware (despite the misleading opaque porcelain) is very rarely afforded the distinction of being finely handpainted in this manner, although Meigh made something of a practice of it for the 1851 Exhibition. A dish such as this has much to recommend it to a commemorative collector. Also it has recently been on view at the Bethnal Green Museum and the more elaborate the pedigree of an object the higher the price tends to be.

£300 — £400

Staffordshire c.1852
Height 8¼ins:20.9cm. No mark
A jug moulded with the titled figure of the Duke of
Wellington surrounded by copper lustre dashes and
scrolls. An uncommon but poorly produced piece, a
crisply moulded and better lustred example £40 — £60.
£18 — £20

Staffordshire 1852
Diameter 6ins:15.3cm. No mark
A child's plate with a technically well engraved portrait
of the aging Duke of Wellington who died in 1852. A
statuette of Napoleon is on the shelf behind his chair.
The same print appears within coloured flower borders
at the same price.

£50 — £80

Staffordshire c.1856
Height 8½ins:21.6cm. No mark
An unusual jug transfer printed in black with two titled
battle scenes of Balaclava and Sebastopol below an
irrelevant border of Grecian ladies emblematic of the
four seasons. The careful and detailed engraving of the
scene is more typical of the Napoleonic Wars than the
cruder treatment of most other items of this date.
Compare with the beaker on p.46.

£100 — £150

A Copeland porcelain tyg commemorating the annexing of the Transvaal during the South African War, 1900. 5½ins:13.7cm. Printed Copeland. £100 — £150.

A Doulton beaker commemorating the Golden Jubilee, made interesting by the dedication, 1887. 4ins:10cm. £25 — £35.

Staffordshire 1856
Height 3¾ins.0.3cm. No mark

A very rare beaker of both Crimean War and local interest. The end of the war was declared in April, 1856, and Worksop obviously decided to celebrate the event. The mugs were probably made either for drinking at a party, presumably for children judging by the size, or sold to raise funds for the returning wounded, or possibly both. This example heavily crazed; in good condition, £100 — £120.

£30 — £50

Staffordshire c.1858
Height 6¼ins:15.8cm. No mark

An earthenware jug of exceptionally ugly form but bearing an uncommon black transfer print of the Princess Royal and the Crown Prince Frederick of Prussia, who were married in 1858. The reverse shows a view of the German royal palace. The squiggly lines are in blue and copper lustre.

£40 — £60

W.T. Copeland c.1860
Plate, diameter 9ins:23cm. Tile, width 8ins:20.2cm. Printed name

Two examples of the same brown transfer print used in different ways within a blue border. The subject is Albert Richard Smith (1816-60) an early contributor to *Punch* and author of several novels including *Christopher Tadpole* who presented illustrated lectures in the Egyptian Hall in Piccadilly. Both plate and plaque, which are uncommon, were sold in the foyer of the theatre.

Plate, £50 — £80
Tile, £60 — £90

Staffordshire 1862
Height 3ins:7.6cm. No mark
An earthenware mug transfer printed in green with a view of the 1862 International Exhibition.
£25 — £40

David Methven and Sons c.1863
Height 7¾ins:19.8cm. Printed initials
An earthenware jug, from an uncommon factory, made for the marriage of Albert Edward, Prince of Wales, to Princess Alexandra of Denmark. The unrecognisable portraits are crudely transfer printed in brown.
£40 — £60

William Brownfield c.1863
Height 7½ins:19.1cm. Registration of design
A Parian jug made to commemorate the wedding of Albert Edward, Prince of Wales, and Princess Alexandra of Denmark at St. George's Chapel, Windsor, on the 10th of March, 1863. The moulded arms are those of the Danish royal family and the Prince's own, the moulding picked out in maroon and yellow. One of the most attractive and well designed jugs of the period, it was probably made over a long period as the quality varies considerably. One of the best of the many variations in colouring is the simple addition of a yellowish-khaki ground. Price can vary from £5 for a poor example to perhaps £40 — £60 for a fine specimen in prime state with its original pewter cover. This example with cover £20 — £25.
£15 — £20

Staffordshire c.1868
Height 3½ins:8.8cm. No mark

An earthenware mug transfer printed with black print of Bright on one side and Gladstone on the other probably made for the elections in November 1868 to help Bright. He was returned and became President of the Board of Trade. A crude production and singularly unattractive, hence, no doubt, its rarity. John Bright had formed with six others the anti-Corn Law Association in Manchester in 1838. Good example £40 — £60.

£10 — £15

Unknown, probably 1882
Height 14ins:35.5cm. Impressed name

A Parian bust of H.W. Longfellow the poet, who died in 1882, well cast and titled at the rear. There is a growing market for literary busts and associated material from book and manuscript collectors which has recently pushed up the price of similar figures.

£80 — £120

Doulton and Co., Lambeth 1883
Height 6½ins:16.5cm. Impressed rosette and date

A commemorative stoneware tyg made for the Egyptian Campaign of 1882-84, the white relief on a sage ground. An uncommon piece and with a contemporary silver mount, Birmingham 1883, helping the price.

£60 — £80

Staffordshire 1883
Diameter 11⅞ins:30.3cm. No mark

A freely painted earthenware plaque of theatrical interest. The portrait is that of Ellen Terry in the part of Beatrice, inscribed on the ribbon at the right, and is painted by Jane M. Rogers, signed and dated London 1883. It was exhibited at Smith & Sons' Art Pottery Exhibition in 1883 and was then priced at 10 guineas. The dress worn in the portrait is now in the Ellen Terry Museum in Small Hythe, near Tenterden, Kent. It is extraordinary that pieces of such interest and quality can still fetch relatively little.

£40 — £60

Doulton and Co., Lambeth 1884
Height 7¾ins:19.7cm.
Impressed name, initials and date

A saltglaze stoneware jug applied with a white portrait of General Gordon and dated inscriptions and quotes from high spots in his career. An almost identical jug was issued the next year after his death in 1885, and reissued in 1895 and 1905, same price. Although semi-mass produced these sprigged jugs and mugs do vary in quality, often the portrait is brown flecked and/or crazed. A really clean, crisp example £60 — £80.

£40 — £60

Staffordshire c.1886
Height 7¾ins:19.8cm. No mark

An earthenware jug probably made to commemorate the death of Fred Archer in 1886. The poorly moulded body is washily coloured, the whole having an amateur quality. Fred Archer was a remarkable jockey winning the Derby five times, the Oaks four and the St. Leger six amongst others in his short career spanning the years 1870 to 1886 when he committed suicide. A rare Staffordshire figure of the same jockey is also recorded, £100 — £150.

£15 — £25

Johnson Brothers, Hanley 1887
Diameter 10ins:25.5cm. Elaborate printed mark

One of the numerous slight and uninteresting plates made for the Golden Jubilee of 1887, this with a colour print portrait of an unamused Victoria. The mark showed five factories and Johnson Bros., Manufacturers of New Royal Semi-porcelain Sanitary Ware. Comparable mugs and jugs from the 1887 Jubilee are generally 10-20% higher in price than those for the following Diamond Jubilee pieces.

£20 — £30

Sunderland c.1890
Diameter 8ins:20.3cm. No mark

A plate printed and coloured with the figure of Jack Crawford, the hero of Camperdown, nailing Admiral Duncan's flag to the mast of the *Venerable* on the 11th October 1797. The border in pink splashed lustre. It is possible that this plate commemorates the erection of Jack Crawford's statue in Mobray Park, Sunderland in 1890.

£35 — £50

Staffordshire 1897
Height 3ins:7.6cm
Printed William Whiteley, London (retailer)

An uncommon mug with a pink transfer commemorating the longest reign in English history. This mug follows the tradition of commemorative wares much more closely than the majority of Diamond Jubilee pieces. Indeed, the moulds for the handle were probably made in the 1840s or 50s. The single colour transfer has a great deal more in common with the Coronation mug on p.41 than the other Jubilee mug, following. A collector of commemorative wares might well find himself drawn to this as a representative example rather than the more colourful latter.

£40 — £60

Robinson & Leadbeater 1897
Height 21ins:53.4cm. No mark

The unusually large size and sharp modelling makes this an expensive piece. The reverse is inscribed to commemorate the sixty years of Victoria's reign, 1837-97.

£80 — £120

Staffordshire 1897
Height 3ins:7.6cm. No mark

A poorly printed celebration of the Diamond Jubilee which can be found in black, green, red or blue. The reverse bears a view of a Royal residence.

£6 — £8

Staffordshire 1897
Diameter of saucer 5ins:12.8cm. No mark

Common, as are the pieces from the 1887 Jubilee. Not, however, as common as the non-event of 1937, the Coronation of Edward VIII. Mugs, plates and cups and saucers from the Coronation of 1902 to that of the present Queen in 1953 are all of little value, £2 — £10 at present, due to the vast numbers surviving.

£2 — £3

Doulton & Co., Lambeth 1897
Height 5ins:12.7cm. Impressed name

A stoneware beaker made for the Diamond Jubilee, the blue body moulded with sage-green portraits of the young and old queen and the dates 1837 and 1897. Originally part of a lemonade-set, with another beaker and jug, £100 — £150.

£15 — £20

Doulton and Co., Lambeth 1897
Height 6½ins:16.4cm. Impressed name

A stoneware tyg commemorating the same event as the jug below. Tygs are normally more expensive than jugs but this example is not as well moulded or coloured.

£50 — £80

Doulton and Co., Lambeth 1900
Height 8¼ins:20.9cm. Impressed name

An uncommon stoneware jug made to commemorate the hoisting of the Flag at Pretoria on 5th June, 1900, and so inscribed.

£50 — £80

Staffordshire c.1900
8¼ins. x 7¾ins:20.9cm x 19.7cm. No mark
A plaque transfer printed with a portrait of Lord
Roberts, the moulded rim green and gilt flecked. A
product appearing better in the photograph than in
reality, the crudely sponged rim colour is typical of
many wares of the turn of the century. Other plaques
from the same series feature Baden Powell, Lt. Gen. Sir
George White, Lord Kitchener or General Macdonald;
all of whom were involved in the South African wars.
£10 — £15

Staffordshire 1902
Diameter 9½ins:24.4cm. Registration of design
A must for collectors of West Islingtoniana but well
down the list for collectors of general Royal
Commemoratives. The green printed outline design is ill
conceived and judging from its position on the plate was
probably engraved for a larger plate with a border.
Typical of numerous 'personalised' commemoratives
made for local distribution.
£8 — £10

Royal Doulton c.1905
Height 8ins:20.3cm
Impressed lion, crown and circle
A stoneware jug commemorating the centenary of the
death of Nelson, his portrait between moulded sea
battles in sage green on a deep blue ground.
£40 — £60

53

Copeland 1910
Height 7¼ins:18.4cm. Shield, name and retailer
One of an edition of one hundred for sale through Thomas Good's to commemorate the death of Edward VII. The printed design brightly coloured and gilt, the figure of Peace on the reverse. Several factories in the 20th century have produced limited commemorative editions for various coronations and other events, generally speaking they have proved a poor investment, most selling in the £40 — £60 region.

£80 — £120

Royal Doulton, Lambeth 1910-1914
Height 7ins:17.8cm
Impressed name and registration of design
A successful revival of an old style spirit flask in the original material, salt-glazed stoneware, modelled by Leslie Harradine. This in the form of the Rt. Hon. John Burns, M.P., representative of Battersea 1892-1918. There are six in the set, Richard Haldane, Herbert Asquith, Arthur Balfour, David Lloyd George and Austin Chamberlain. Set £380 — £400.
£40 — £60

Royal Doulton, Burslem 1911
Diameter 10½ins:26.7cm. Printed lion, circle mark
A good earthenware plate for the 1911 Coronation, of high standard as were all Doulton products at this date. The design is well conceived and printed in clear, bright colours.

£30 — £40

Staffordshire 1919
Height
4½ins. and 2¾ins.
11.4cm and 7cm
No mark
Two examples of First World War Peace celebration mugs, the one shown on the right commissioned for a local event. Compare with the Crimea Peace baker on p.46.

£2 — £3 each

Royal Doulton 1936
Height 10¼ins:26cm
Printed lion and circle, inscription
An earthenware loving cup designed by Charles Noke which should be accompanied by a certificate signed by him. The base bears a long inscription and the number of the piece from an edition of 2,000. Condition is important with 2,000 about. They are not expensive at the moment but they have a good chance of rising dramatically in price in the next few years. The certificate at the present time makes little difference to the price; should there be a rise, then that difference will be increased. A similar mug was made for the 1911 Coronation and the one illustrated was adapted to show George VI and Queen Elizabeth for their Coronation in 1937. All at present fetch about the same price. This is probably the most desirable of the abortive Edward VIII Coronation pieces. Ordinary mugs, plates, cups, etc. are extremely common and are in the region of £5 — £15 per piece.

£100 — £150

Wedgwood 1951
Height 3ins:7.6cm. Printed name
A now uncommon mug printed in black with appropriately futuristic designs for the Festival of Britain, 1951. The illustrated side featuring the Dome of Discovery and the Skylon, the reverse with the 1851 Crystal Palace building. This, and other commemorative pieces of the 1940s and 1950s must have a good chance of rising quickly in price in the near future.

£20 — £30

A Staffordshire figure of Lucrezia, c.1810. 10ins:25.5cm. £80 — £120.

A Moore Brothers Liu Hai's toad with glass eyes, c.1880. 7¼ins:18.5cm. Impressed Moore and T. Goode and Co. £25 — £35.

Figures, Busts and Animals

Except for the Staffordshire figures which are dealt with in a separate section, earthenware was not much used for the production of human forms, probably because of the lack of detail obtainable. Porcelain was much better suited to the purpose until the bolder modelling and bright colouration of majolica arrived on the scene. It is, however entirely appropriate to the simpler forms of the animal kingdom and there are collectors who are interested in nothing else. The earlier models, such as the bull baiting groups and the lustred cats, have long been appreciated. The later dogs trace their genealogy back to the Chinese Buddhist lions. No self respecting "antique" shop is complete without several, however recent their pedigree, and they are still lapped up by an unsuspecting public. Remember, if the dog is earthenware, it is not Rockingham: if it has shredded clay fur, it is not Rockingham. What is more, some are fakes.

Staffordshire c.1800
Height 3ins:7.6cm. No mark
A small crouching lion, simply cast with gaping jaws. The price given is for a yellow glazed example. In green £70 — £100; clear £40 — £60.
£120 — £150

Pratt c.1800
Height 7¼ins:18.4cm. No mark
A highly stylised lion (or is it a leopard with those spots?) in the typical Pratt colours of yellow, brown, black and ochre, the base with green leaves. It could have been made at any date between 1790 and 1810.
£400 — £500

Staffordshire c.1810-1815
Height 12ins:30.5cm. No mark

This lion is covered overall with a splashed pink lustre, his eyebrows and whiskers black. Pink lustre is a great deal more easy to date than copper or silver — the splashing is the give-away. In addition this particular piece had a good pedigree, having been sold at Sotheby's in 1947. Any such recorded history will considerably add to the value of a piece, particularly if the previous collection was a prestigious one.

£700 — £800

Sunderland/Staffordshire 1810-1830
Height 6½ins:16.5cm. No mark

A very rare splashed pink lustre cat. Although crudely moulded, its face is more like that of a pig than a cat. A few pink-lustre animals exist and cats are more desirable than most.

£700 — £900

Walton early 19th century
Height 5¾ins:14.8cm. Impressed name

A pair of royal supporters, the lion and unicorn at rest below the stylised bocage (literally woodland) which is typical of the period. They were possibly made at the time of George IV's accession or coronation. Amusing animal groups, particularly cuddly lions, are always popular.

£300 — £400

Staffordshire early 19th century
Height 8¼ins:20.9cm. No mark
A naïvely modelled and coloured leopard
resting on a dark green base.
£150 — £250

Staffordshire early 19th century
Height 8½ins:21.6cm. No mark
A large and rare model of a goat, the
horns brown, and on a brown, green and
yellow base.
£300 — £350

Staffordshire early 19th century
Height 10½ins:26.7cm. No mark
A large and simply modelled cow with
brown patched hide standing in front of a
stump.

£250 — £350

Staffordshire c.1820
Height 16¼ins:41.3cm. No mark

A rare and large earthenware black stallion, very much in the Leeds tradition. These horses were made for saddlers' shop windows as display material in both the late 18th and early 19th centuries. This particular model has misfired and the black enamel is matt in places or is flaking off. Good example, £800 — £1,200.

£600 — £900

Probably Fulham c.1820
Height 6ins:15cm. No mark

A stoneware relief of no easily definable purpose, crudely but vigorously cast as St. George and the Dragon under a yellowish-brown salt-glaze.

£20 — £25

Obadiah Sherrat c.1825
Height 9¾ins:24.8cm. No mark

A boldly modelled bull-baiting group, the bull tossing one dog while another attacks its head. Typical of Sherrat's modelling, as is the footed base, in this case sponged with green enamel. Restored example (as most are) £300 — £400.

£400 — £450

Staffordshire c.1835
Height 11½ins:29.2cm. No mark
A good pair of lions, well modelled and coloured in ochre, based on Renaissance bronze originals. This pair made more unusual by the ball under the fore-paw being turned into a globe. The ball has come down from Chinese mythology when the Buddhist lions or dogs-of-fo (or shi-shi in Japanese) were represented with a pup for the female and a brocade ball for the male. These household guardians were brought back to this country by travellers in the 18th century and were much copied both as lions and as dogs, hence the numerous spaniels.
£150 — £180

John Lloyd, Shelton c.1840
Height 9½ins and 10¼ins:24.1 and 26cm. Impressed name
These two earthenware spaniels sum up all that Staffordshire dogs should be: compare them with those on p.67. Not quite a pair, their fur formed from shredded clay and with wonderfully blank expressions. Particularly interesting for the impressed mark which is very rare. Unmarked pair £120 — £150.
£180 — £220

Possibly Glasgow c.1840
Height 26½ins:67.2cm
Impressed Chadwick, Baker and Co, Sheffield
A massive stoneware eagle, probably made as a shop or garden ornament. The name is most likely that of the retailer, as no maker of that name is recorded.
£180 — £200

Minton 1865
Height 71¼ins:181cm
Impressed name and date code
A superb pair of earthenware figures of blackamoors shown at the 1862 Exhibition. Well modelled and brilliantly coloured, supporting a flat-topped basket which may have been intended to carry a jardinière. Figures of this size, nearly six feet in height overall, are extremely rare and decorative, justifying the high price.
£5,000 — £8,000

Staffordshire c.1870-1880
Height 11¼ins:28.6cm. No mark
An amusingly slinky greyhound with a hare, but very common and not much sought after. Should be a pair; £60 — £80. Smaller size pro rata.
£20 — £30

Minton 1872
Height 7½ins:19cm
Impressed Minton and date code
An amusing earthenware group of two shi-shi (Japanese Buddhist lions or dogs-of-fo) fighting. Brightly coloured in blue and manganese after a contemporary Kutani original

£30 — £50

Royal Worcester c.1875
Height 7½ins:19cm. Impressed crowned circle
Royal Worcester earthenware of this type is not common and, despite being of unusually good quality, is not highly priced. Restoration is particularly difficult to spot on these models which, being of soft earthenware, are prone to damage.
£100 — £150

Staffordshire c.1887
Height 9½ins:24.1cm. No mark
The royal supporters flanking a watch face, possibly originally an advertising display. Sparsely decorated but with some charm, desirable as a centrepiece to a pair of royal figures. With more elaborate decoration £50 — £80.

£20 — £30

Staffordshire c.1880-1900
Height 11¾ins:29.8cm
No mark
One of a pair of stag hunt spill holders, coloured dull brown and green and touched with metallic gilding. Note the sprayed colour on the stag. The mercury gilding indicates a late date. Pair £20 — £30.

£5 — £8

Staffordshire
last quarter of the
19th century
Height 3ins:7.7cm
No mark
A pair of small King Charles spaniels, crudely moulded and coloured. These are being reproduced and can be found in decorators and so-called antique shops where they tend to be more expensive than those of an earlier date.

£20 — £30

A Minton majolica hen bowl after a model by J. Henk, moulded signature. 13ins:33cm.
Impressed Mintons, date code for 1876. £80 — £120.

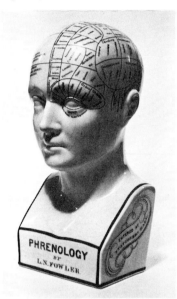

Staffordshire late 19th century
Height 11¼ins:28.6cm
Printed retailer's mark and
testimonial
An earthenware bust marketed by
the phrenologist, L.N. Fowler. It is
little wonder the "science" of
phrenology was abandoned, since a
comparison with the bust on the
right reveals startling discrepancies
in the areas controlling certain
functions. Fowler's bust is the most
frequently met with, and is also the
best manufactured, occasionally
being accompanied by the printed
explanatory booklet which has little
effect on the price. They are much
loved by smart interior decorators
and doctors with a sense of humour.
£70 — £100

Staffordshire late 19th century
Height 5½ins:14cm. No mark
Another earthenware bust, unusual for
being in the form of an inkwell and pen
holder. The base is impressed "By F.
Bridges, Phrenologist".
£40 — £60

Staffordshire late 19th century
Height 6ins:15.2cm. No mark
An earthenware cow creamer after an 18th century
original in silver. The cream was poured in the back,
which now lacks its cover, and issued through the open
mouth. The price given is for this example with cracked
legs and chips, but even a perfect example of such a bad
model would still only be £3 — £5. Earlier, better
examples, up to £100.
£2 — £3

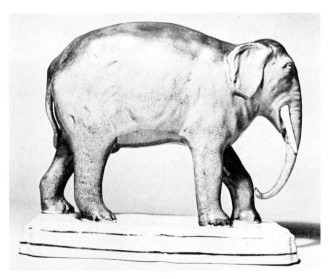

Staffordshire late 19th century
Height 11ins:27.9cm. No mark
An anonymous brown-speckled elephant; not Jumbo,
since interest in him had died with him many years
before this example. Nevertheless elephants are rare and
this is a good specimen.
£80 — £120

**Staffordshire
late 19th/early 20th
century
Height 3¼ins:8.2cm**

A pair of poodles with shredded clay fur, a basket in each maw, bright-blue base, gilt line. It is almost impossible from the photograph to determine the date but the poor quality gilt-lining, lack of wear on the underside of the almost porcelain-like body and strange smeared glaze, indicate a late date for these dogs, which are normally sold as mid-19th century. They are probably being produced today. Early examples £70 — £100.

£20 — £30

**Staffordshire c.1900
Height 7¼ins:18.5cm. No mark**

Another cow creamer but with cover, poorly modelled with blue transfer-printed body, green leaf-moulded base and tinted face.

£10 — £15

**Royal Doulton, Lambeth c.1930
Height 4ins:10.2cm
Impressed lion, crown and circle**

A stoneware pelican pin tray glazed in blue, pink and green, and of more interest to collectors of Art and Studio Pottery. A large number of different small dressing-table, desk and mantelpiece ornaments in the form of birds, animals and humans were produced by the factory before and in the twenty years after the First World War, and interest in these is growing.

£50 — £70

Staffordshire c.1930
Height 4½ins to 9ins:11.4cm to 22.8cm. No mark

A set of ten characters from the Alice books, simply moulded and brightly coloured, each with the printed identification on the base. They do not fall specifically into any ceramic collecting category but might join a collection of children's books or related material.

£180 — £220

Robert Heron, Wemyss 1930s
Length 11ins:27.9cm
Painted "Nekola pinxit" and
retailer's mark

A squat pig painted with thistles by Joseph Nekola and signed by him on the base, which raises the price from the £100 — £150 level. Variations in design include roses and black patches and the ground colours vary, affecting the price considerably: dark blue, very rare, £400 — £500; yellow, rare, £300 — £500; plain colours rarer still. An earlier example which would be impressed Wemyss and RHS and therefore Scottish, double. A larger version at 16½ins. (41.9cm) would be £200 — £300.

£150 — £250

Jugs, Mugs,
Loving Cups and Goblets

During the eighteenth and first half of the nineteenth century the jug was one of the most important household utensils. Milk and ale would both be fetched and kept in it, as would water for the table. It was natural that it would be singled out for special treatment and elaborate moulded and painted decoration can be found throughout the century apart from the usual underglaze-blue print. The jug and loving cup or tyg (with two or three handles) was also the most common dedicated gift; there was obviously a flourishing trade in special orders to celebrate marriages, births and engagements, along with the occasional "thank you" present to a local dignitary, mine or factory owner from his workmen. These are rare, probably because most of these gifts were in silver. They are generally dated and often bear the name of town or village. These are now much sought after and no doubt find their way back to the local antique shop for sale to a member of the community. The jugs from the first quarter of the nineteenth century can be found with fine silver lustre decoration and these have been appreciated for a considerable period, articles on collecting lustre jugs appearing in magazines seventy years ago. These can now fetch high prices and are particularly desirable with birds and animals and/or yellow grounds.

In the late 1830s and '40s the moulded jug held sway, first made in stoneware and then in parian, some after designs by the best designers of the day. As the century wore on, so did the moulds and the quality degenerates. The majolica artists of the second half of the century attacked the jug with the same fervour as the rest of the field and a few magnificently original pieces were produced.

With the growth of small kilns and potteries round the country, there is something of a revival of the dedicated mug or jug, usually in the Thomas Toft, slip-trailed tradition.

Staffordshire
First quarter of the 19th century
Height 8½ins:21.6cm. No mark
A dark-brown glazed loving cup, moulded with portraits of Nelson between lions and snakes, the whole of dreary aspect. The interior has two frogs.
£70 — £90

Staffordshire 1810-1815
Height 3¼ins:8.3cm. No mark
A small and attractive yellow ground jug, with silver resist vine leaves and iron-red tendrils.
£160 — £180

Possibly Fulham
First half of the 19th century
Height 6¼ins:16cm. No mark

An uncommon object, beer mugs being a much more appropriate utensil to manufacture in heavy stoneware than goblets. Some research is being done into the variations in the mould of the smoking figure, the presence of a bird in the tree, etc. Thus it is hoped to be able to attribute the pieces to specific factories.

£20 — £25

Staffordshire 1810-1820
Height 6½ins:16.5cm. No mark

An attractive silver lustre jug with a mother bird feeding a fledgling below fruiting vine. A good subject and well executed. Same on a canary-yellow ground, £400 — £500.

£80 — £120

Staffordshire 1810-1820
Height 5¼ins:13.3cm. No mark

A very unusual jug with a bird print in sepia reserved on a silver lustre ground, the flowers and other details then picked out in coloured enamels.

£400 — £450

Staffordshire 1810-1820
Height 3½ins:9cm. No mark
A small and rare jug printed in blue with titled scenes of
"Women Grinding Corn" and "A Martin on a Rock"
reserved on a silver lustre ground. Not only are titled
prints uncommon but the corn grinding scene is an
accurate picture of country life of the period, the jug
originally being sold mostly to the country folk to whom
it would be an everyday scene.
£200 — £250

Staffordshire c.1815
Height 6½ins:16.5cm. No mark
A silver resist jug with bold flowers, leaves and fruit,
some heightened in bright enamels. The latter is not
common; in silver lustre only, £120 — £150.
£150 — £200

Staffordshire c.1815
Height 4¾ins:12.1cm. No mark
An attractive and rare mug, transfer printed in blue with
a sporting scene after George Morland, below flowers
against a silver ground. The combination of the blue
and silver is particularly effective, but not often seen.
The high price is also helped by the desirability of
sporting subjects, not only in the ceramic field but also
of prints, paintings and equipment.
£380 — £450

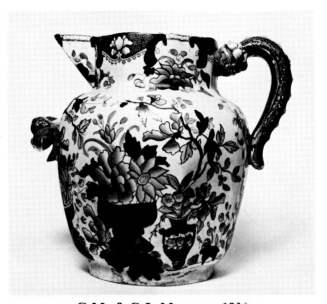

Staffordshire 1816
Height 7ins:17.8cm. No mark
A rare commemorative puzzle jug, well potted with pierced neck, the sides painted in pink lustre with rose sprays, the front with a wreath enclosing the initials TH and the date 1816. Dated pieces always fetch a higher price than undated, for, if genuine, they can be used to date other similar objects and styles. Note the quality of the painting of the wreath and initials.
£200 — £250

G.M. & C.J. Mason c.1820
Height 12ins:30.5cm. Printed crowned pelmet
A large ironstone jug, printed in underglaze blue and brightly enamelled with a vaguely Oriental pattern. The beast mask under the spout is to facilitate lifting and pouring. Slightly cracked example, £50 — £60.
£80 — £120

Staffordshire 1820-1830
Height 4½ins:11.5cm No mark
A goblet based on a glass rummer of around 1815-20. The bladed knop is typical of a great number of glasses of the period. The body is thinly potted and covered in a good splashed pink lustre. Pair, £80 — £100.
£25 — £35

St. Anthony's Pottery c.1825
Height 4ins:10cm approx. Printed triangle device
The St. Anthony's Pottery was in production from about 1780 to 1878 and, since little seems to be marked, attribution is difficult. Each piece of this tea service is transfer printed in black, the bands in pink lustre.
£8 — £10

G.M. & C.J. Mason c.1825
Height 10½ins:26cm. Printed name

A large jug typical of Mason's, with black printed outline and hand coloured in enamels and gilding. The pattern of the Chinese "Eight Precious Objects" and the hundred antiques could have been taken from almost contemporary objects.

£50 — £90

London, Derbyshire, Nottingham c.1830
Height 10¾ins:27.3cm. No mark

An unusually large stoneware jug, probably made for beer or cider in the days when these were collected from the local inn and taken home to consume. More interesting than most as it has the Royal Arms and the landlord's name, Benjamin Poled, Lord Nelson Inn, York Street, Leeds. Without this, £20 — £30.

£30 — £40

Staffordshire c.1830
Height 3ins:7.6cm. No mark

An unusual jug printed in black with girls in various national costumes and appropriately titled. Although uncommon, it does not really fit into a collecting field and is therefore inexpensive.

£10 — £15

Staffordshire c.1830
Height 5¾ins:14.5cm. No mark

An attractively simple, well proportioned jug in biscuit brown with silver lustre borders. Too simple to appeal to many, hence the low price.

£10 — £15

Staffordshire c.1830
Height 3½ins:9cm. No mark

A goblet moulded with arrow head motifs against a green ground, the interior and foot in mottled pink lustre. An unusual but not very attractive object.

£40 — £50

Doulton and Watts, Lambeth 1830
Height 12¾ins:32.3cm
Impressed Doulton and Watts

A salt-glazed stoneware jug of Nelson impressed "Nile 1798" and "Trafalgar 1805". These jugs were probably introduced, but not by Doulton, shortly after Nelson's death at Trafalgar. They were certainly produced throughout the century, not only in this size, but also smaller. So many variations in quality and size occur that the price can range upwards of £15.

£200 — £250

Staffordshire 1831
Height 7½ins:19.1cm. No mark

An earthenware jug transfer printed in blue with a landscape and hand painted with an inscription. The wide price range is given to indicate the possible effect of conflicting passions where items of local interest come up for sale. This particular jug fetched £50. It is often possible with sufficient information to trace from the census returns at the Public Record Office the actual house, who lived there, and what work the householder was engaged in.

£40 — £200

Samuel and John Burton 1832-1845
Height 7ins:17.8cm. S. & JB on plaque
A well moulded jug of ugly form from a rare factory.
The piece is made more unusual by details such as the
scrolls and the gilt rim. An interesting and cheap
collection could be formed by picking a period of say
fifteen years and collecting an example from all the
Staffordshire potteries then working.
£4 — £6

Staffordshire/Sunderland/Wales c.1835
Height 6ins:15.2cm. No mark
This copper lustre jug has a further coloured enamel
band with pink lustre berries making it slightly unusual
and more desirable. Pink lustre has always been
traditionally attributed to Sunderland but it was
certainly made elsewhere.
£10 — £15

Staffordshire c.1835
Height 7½ins:19.1cm. No mark
A Mason-type ironstone jug, naïvely painted in bright
enamels and gilding. A marked Mason example, which
would be of better quality, would be £20 — £30 and a
graduated set of five, £150 — £250.
£5 — £10

Elkin, Knight and Bridgewood c.1835
Height 10½ins:26.7cm. Printed mark initials
An underglaze-blue transfer printed jug with a
sacrificial scene. A well produced piece from a small
factory.
£18 — £20

A Staffordshire pearlware jug printed and hand coloured, c.1815.
5ins:12.8cm. £30 — £40.

A Staffordshire canary-yellow mug and jug, one with a
black print and silver lustre bands, the other with silver
lustre resist leaves, c.1815. 5½ins. and 3ins:14cm and
7.5cm. £60 — £80 and £200 — £300.

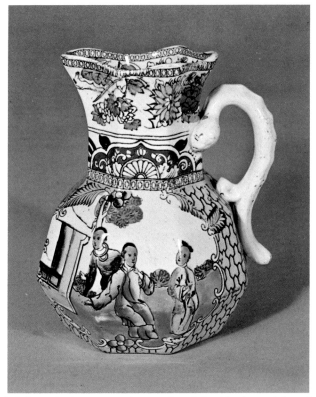

A Mason's ironstone jug, printed in black and hand
coloured, c.1830. 6¾ins:17cm. Printed ribbon mark.
£35 — £45.

Davenport 1836
Height 12¼ins:31cm
Impressed name, anchor and date

A rare Martha Gunn earthenware jug from a factory that made few figures, the woman enamelled in flesh tints with yellow hat and black dress. The most interesting point is the presence of the date which helps to place comparable jugs.

£40 — £60

Wales/Sunderland/Staffordshire c.1840
Height 3¼ins:8.3cm. No mark

An almost miniature copper lustre jug with white and coloured flowers. Copper and silver lustres were originally developed as the poor man's gold and silver and seems to have been particularly popular in Wales. The copper is in fact formed by a layer of the metallic oxide turning back to metal by the firing.

£8 — £10

Staffordshire c.1840
Height 5¾ins:14.6cm. No mark

A black basalt jug in imitation of Wedgwood but lacking the quality. Possibly made around 1837 since the national emblems are incorporated in the moulded scrollwork. Typical of quantities of non-Wedgwood basalt and imitation basalt made in the first half of the century, little of which is in much demand.

£12 — £15

Staffordshire c.1840
Height 5ins:12.5cm. No mark
A silver lustre jug moulded with flutes and based on a contemporary silver shape. The wear is acceptable and being very soft a perfect example is highly unlikely, not to say suspicious.
£8 — £10

Staffordshire/Sunderland c.1840
Height 6¾ins:17cm. No mark
A jug simply painted with stylised flower panels but with pink lustre rim and detailed handle. Typical of many moulded and painted jugs of the period, the price depending on the decorative qualities. This example is pleasantly restrained; worse painting, £4 — £8, better, £15 — £40.
£10 — £15

Staffordshire c.1840
Height 9¼ins:23.5cm. No mark
A curious earthenware loving cup transfer printed in blurred black and touched with colour, with scenes of a meeting inscribed "The Real Cabinet of Friendship, Justice and Equity, Every man helped his Neighbour". Quite what the scene depicts and what the cup was made for remains a mystery. It was probably commissioned by one of the numerous friendly societies that grew up in the first half of the 19th century.
£30 — £50

W. Ridgway, Son and Co. c.1840
Height 11ins:27.9cm. Pressed name and date

A good stoneware jug, fine enough to be parian, moulded with jousting knights probably inspired by the Eglington Tournament in 1839. Not only is this a good clean example but it is of large size and the original Britannia metal cover in pristine condition. This example in buff but it can be found in parian and in pale blue, green and white, the variations making little difference to the price. Smaller example £20 — £30, poorly moulded or discoloured specimens down to £8 — £10. If there is no cover, the presence of holes in the mouth would seem to indicate that one is missing, but it seems possible that covers were an optional extra. However, the same jug with a cover is obviously more desirable than one with holes only and is more expensive. It seems unlikely, despite the frequent appearance of grape vine in the design, that the jugs were made for fetching ale from the local public house as their size, usually about a pint to two pints, would seem to rule against this. More likely they were for milk, the cover helping to keep out dirt and flies, the decoration being simply decoration.

£50 — £60

J. & R. Godwin c.1845
Height 4ins:10.2cm. Printed initials

A fairly common railway item with the "Fury" pulling three carriages printed in brown with hand colouring. The dating of these railway pieces is extremely difficult and the presence of a factory mark makes some difference to the price, an unmarked example £25 — £35. The same print of a train pulling carriages through a landscape can be found with different names on the engine including Jaco and Wooda, shown on the right. The price is not affected.

£30 — £50

J. & R. Godwin c.1845
Height 4ins:10.2cm. No mark

An extremely crude earthenware mug transfer printed in brown and illogically coloured in maroon and green with blobs of enamel over the steam engine Wooda, which, as can be seen, is the same print with the name changed as the example shown on the left. Good example, £30 — £50.

£20 — £30

Sunderland 1848
Height 9ins:22.8cm. No mark

A good pink lustre jug printed in black with the Iron Bridge and a Masonic verse, the front with a print of the Mariner's Arms and a dedicatory inscription dated 1848. The date here makes the difference between the price given and £70 — £90. Less good prints or lustring, from £30.

£100 — £150

Staffordshire mid-19th century
Height 4¾ins:12.1cm. No mark

An earthenware loving cup transfer printed in black with the pseudo armorial of the Loyal Order of Ancient Shepherds Ashton Unity, Established 1826. The scene above the date depicts a strange scene of a woman and three (starving?) children fleeing from a man with a flag into the arms of a woman on a cornucopia, presumably Charity, the whole taking place in a graveyard. Who is the man with the flag? The collector building up a history of the numerous Orders of the time would have an endless source of amusement sorting out the allegorical significance of the sheep, beehives, praying groups, harps and so on that appear in the prints.

£20 — £25

Staffordshire/Sunderland mid-19th century
Height 6½ins:16.4cm

An earthenware loving cup transfer printed in brown with a landscape touched with colours on a blue ground. The interior is applied with a frog. Apparently in the 19th century, ale was of such murky consistency that the unsuspecting imbiber would only notice the amphibian as he drained his brew, no doubt much to the amusement of the lookers-on.

£10 — £15

Staffordshire mid-19th century
Height 2¾ins:12cm. No mark

A small child's mug naïvely printed in black with a woman on a donkey. Now being sought after for their charm and will probably rise quickly over the next few years.

£8 — £12

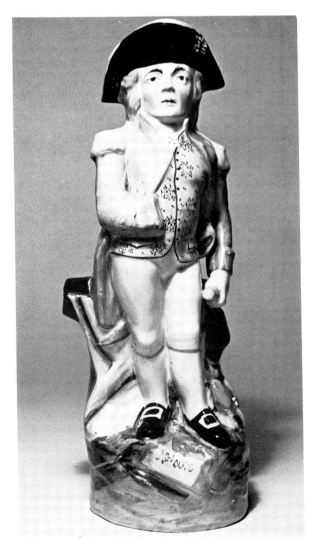

Hackwood mid-19th century
Height 4¼ins:10.8cm. Impressed Hackwood

An unusual soda water cup, the pale blue earthenware body transfer printed in black with the retailer's name and directions for use. The interior is made in two sections, one for water and one for the powder; on raising the cup and drinking, the two mixed in the mouth or stomach releasing quantities of carbon dioxide. The use of the word Elaboratory instead of Laboratory is interesting, since it was already archaic by the early 19th century and its usage here was probably to lend a spurious pedigree, hence the Royal Coat of Arms and the prominence of the establishment date. The high price is a reflection of the interest of collectors of medical pottery and other equipment, many of them in the profession.

£40 — £50

Sunderland c.1850
Height 4ins:10.2cm

An uninteresting little mug, transfer printed in black with a sentimental rhyme. Hand lustred in pink. This example somewhat worn, but a good example is still only £12 to £15.

£8 — £12

Staffordshire c.1850
Height 11½ins:29.3cm. No mark

A late and badly coloured jug in the form of Nelson, shakily titled on a reserve on the base.

£25 — £35

Staffordshire second half of the 19th century
Height 5¾ins:14.5cm. No mark
A blue and white jug attractively printed in underglaze blue with two children in a garden and the Royal Coat of Arms. The print was obviously engraved in the 1820s but the wide crackle of the glaze suggests a later date, although it is difficult to decide when during the second half of the century it might have been made.

£10 — £15

Staffordshire/Sunderland
Second half of the 19th century
Height 8½ins:21.6cm. No mark
A loving cup of atrocious quality, badly moulded with a spaniel and a game bird, the enamel colour being so badly applied that the dog appears to be wading through a sea of mud. The interior also with a frog. These cups are very common and not much sought after.

£8 — £10

Staffordshire c.1860
Height 14¾ins:37.4cm. No mark
A rare and large earthenware jug transfer printed in black and hand coloured with numerous unrelated prints, the most interesting being the named figure of "Cashmore — Everybody's Clown". Joe Cashmore, fl.1860, specialised in acrobatics and stilt walking. The animals on the jug are based on wood engravings by Thomas Bewick in his *General History of Quadrupeds*. The pictorial roundels at the mouth are prints made for children's plates.

£150 — £200

Doulton & Co. c.1860
Height 9ins:22.8cm. Impressed Doulton, Lambeth
A stoneware jug, probably from an earlier Doulton & Watts mould, with dogs hunting stags or boar, the handle as an oak branch, the whole glazed in two tones of brown. Apart from the unattractive subjects a good and desirable object and unusual at this period for being marked. Unmarked example, £30 — £35.

£40 — £60

Minton 1861
Height 14½ins:36.8cm.
Impressed name, and date code
A good ewer from a model by Hughues Protat with his monogram under the handle. The body crisply cast under green and brown glazes, the putti cream. Protat was a French sculptor who designed majolica and parian for Minton and also taught at the Hanley and Stoke Schools of Design from 1850-64. He left Minton in 1858 for Wedgwood.

£70 — £100

Sunderland 1862
Height 9¼ins:23.4cm. No mark
A good jug with a titled Crimea print on one side and "The Sailor's Farewell" on the other, made additionally interesting by an inscription dated 1862. Without inscription, £60 — £70.

£80 — £100

Staffordshire 1867
Height 7ins:18cm. No mark

An interesting presentation tankard inscribed "Presented to Mr. John Clarke, Underground Manager of Strangewayhall Colliery, 1867" in gilding on the reverse, the plum ground with gilt stars. These inscribed pieces have been rising in price recently and will probably go faster than most. This example perhaps more slowly as it is in pottery, more unusual than porcelain but not so desirable.

£60 — £80

Minton 1870
Height 14¼ins:36.3cm
Impressed name and date code

A good majolica ewer from a model by Hughues Protat with his initials under the handle, the shell body and figures in restrained polychrome.

£180 — £200

Wales/Staffordshire/Sunderland c.1870
Height 2¾ins:7cm. No mark

A small copper lustre mug crudely daubed with leaves on a blue band. Typical of thousands of others.

£6 — £8

Salopian/Staffordshire 1870s
Height 3¾ins:8.3cm. No mark
A loving cup with Clifton Suspension Bridge in black transfer. Of late date and, therefore, much less interesting than a contemporary example.

£8 — £10

Staffordshire 1875
Height 6¾ins:17.3cm. No mark
An unusual loving cup transfer printed in black with scenes of the "Music Hall, Scarborough. From the Sands" and the "Spa Saloon and Italian Terrace, Scarborough", below the painted inscription. This is an early example of holiday resort pottery. The interior has two frogs.

£25 — £35

Staffordshire last quarter of the century
Height 7½ins:19.1cm. No mark
An amusing mug transfer printed in puce with a dreadful accident between two lady cyclists, recording what must have been a not uncommon event of the period.

£35 — £45

Doulton & Co., Lambeth 1876
Height 9ins:22.8cm. Impressed circular name
A stoneware jug in the form of a blue sphinx, the mouth silver mounted. More of interest to collectors of studio pottery.

£60 — £90

85

Doulton & Co. 1880
Height 9½ins:24.1cm
Impressed circle mark dated 1880

A stoneware lemonade jug, well sprigged with cricketers, the handle in the form of bat and stumps, the mouth silver mounted, Birmingham 1881, which adds to the value. Without, £100 — £120. All the stoneware Doulton sporting subjects are sought after, not only by Doulton collectors, but also by devotees of the relevant pastime. They were originally no doubt used for refreshment during the various events and also given as prizes. Doulton would undertake special orders with appropriate inscriptions. Set complete with two beakers, £300 — £400.

£120 — £180

Doulton & Co. 1898
Heights 5½ins to 7¼ins:14cm to 18.5cm. Impressed name

Three graduated saltglaze stoneware jugs each applied with white bucolic reliefs, the rims silver mounted by W. Hutton and Sons Ltd., London, 1898. Many of these very common jugs, made from the 18th to the 20th centuries, were made to take mounts but this was presumably at the discretion of the retailer who apparently had them mounted by his nearest silversmith. There seems no other reason for the number of Sheffield and Birmingham assay marks.

£50 — £60

Sunderland/Staffordshire c.1900
Height 6½ins:16.4cm. No mark

A dreadful copper lustre jug, the brightly and crudely painted fruit reserved on the copper ground, the neck moulded with vine. Probably cast from c.1840 moulds between 1900 and the First World War and lacking the naïve appeal of the original. Compare with p.75.

£7 — £10

Doulton c.1900
Height 5¾ins:15cm. Impressed name

An attractive mug with the same reliefs as those on the three pieces below, here set between the blue flowers. Although produced in quite large quantities, crisply moulded examples in good condition are popular, mainly with collectors of transport material, not collectors of Doulton studio pottery.

£50 — £70

Doulton & Co. c.1900
Heights 4¾ins and 8ins
12cm and 20.4cm
Impressed Doulton

A lemonade set, the buff body with white reliefs titled "Military", "Road" and "Path", referring to the uses to which the safety bicycle could be put. It is, as usual, silver mounted, the mounts with year letters for 1901 and 1902. The different years do not necessarily mean a married set; the pieces might well have been sent in a large batch for mounting, some bearing the letter for the end of one year and some the beginning of the next. As far as the assay offices are concerned the new year starts in May when the letters are changed.

£100 — £150

Wemyss early 20th century
Height 11ins:27.9cm. Painted name
A jug moulded as a sailor in blue jacket. A very
badly produced object selling for a high price
because of its name.
£100 — £200

Sunderland 20th century
Height 5¾ins:14.6cm. No mark
A small reproduction jug with a smudgy black print
within a streaky line border, the neck with ugly pink
lustre, painted not splashed on.
£20 — £30

S. Fielding and Co. c.1920
Height 4½ins:11.5cm
Printed name and Crown Devon
A cream glazed mug lightly moulded and coloured with
the figure of John Peel and the printed words to the
tune. The musical box hidden in the base plays when the
mug is raised. Very much part of the ''Olde England''
movement of which the Doulton jugs are a part.
£20 — £30

Royal Doulton, Burslem 1936
Height 10¾ins:27.3cm. Printed lion and crown etc.
One of a series of limited edition moulded earthenware
jugs, designed mainly by Charles Noke with relief
coloured scenes or figures. They have a large devoted
following in the U.S.A., the price depending on the
number in the edition 500 or 1,000, £100 — £250.
£140 — £180

Miscellaneous

In this section can be found some of the vast numbers of pottery objects which do not fit happily into the other categories including some of the more bizzare pieces; the problem has been in selecting which to put in and which to leave out.

Staffordshire early 19th century Height 10½ins:26.8cm No mark

A watch stand supported by a pillar flanked by two children, the hollow receptacle surrounded by green leaves. These holders were made to take fob watches when taken from their owners' pockets at night and were popular up to the third quarter of the century.

£80 — £120

F. & R. Pratt c.1800
Height 4½ins:11.5cm. No mark

A small money box in the form of a house and typically glazed in browns, green and ochre. Compare with the fake on p.235. These money boxes and pastille burners are generally considered as late 18th century but some would appear to be considerably later, probably cast from the same moulds.

£70 — £100

Staffordshire first half of the 19th century
Length 4ins:10cm. No mark

A miniature cradle, simply moulded with basket-weave, on two rockers. These cradles were made either for children or as a gift at the birth of a child.

£25 — £35

William Fifield, Bristol 1811
Height 4¼ins:11cm. No mark

An interesting and attractive spirit barrel with brown
ribs painted in Pratt browns, green, blue and ochre with
a flower trail, one end incised and coloured Mary Gale
1811. William Fifield and his son were decorators
working on various Bristol wares from about 1810-55,
this therefore being an early example.

£50 — £70

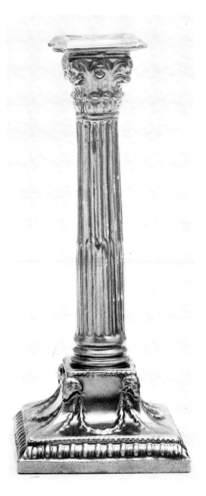

Leeds c.1815
Height 9ins:22.9cm
Impressed Leeds Pottery

A rare candlestick based on a silver
original. The body reasonably well
moulded and under a silver lustre.
A pair would be a very desirable,
£250 — £300.

£50 — £80

Staffordshire c.1815
Height 4¾ins:12cm. No mark

A rare pot-pourri decorated in silver resist with stylised
fruiting vine. An example with restored handle, £80 —
£120. Compare with the Wedgwood marked piece on
p.202.

£300 — £350

Castleford type c.1815-1820
Height 11ins:27.9cm. No mark

A mantelpiece obelisque in porcellaneous stoneware painted to simulate marble above a brightly enamelled scene. Single obelisques are as sad as single candlesticks and really only look well as paperweights on pedestal desks. Pair, £200 — £300.

£30 — £40

G.M. & C.J. Mason 1820-1825
Height 7ins:17.8cm
Impressed patent ironstone mark

A rare letter rack in ironstone, painted in white enamel on the mazarine blue ground with vignettes and gilt scrolls. The painting style follows on from the white enamelling on glass by the Beilby family of Newcastle and connects with the so-called Mary Gregory decoration in the second half of the century.

£60 — £80

G.M. & C.J. Mason c.1830
Height 15ins:38.1cm. Printed crown and scroll

An unusually large canister and cover in ironstone, transfer printed in black and hand coloured in famille rose enamels with a mandarin design. The pattern is based on a Chinese original dating from c.1780. The cover is broken on this example. Perfect, £180 — £220.

£120 — £140

G.M. & C.J. Mason c.1825
Height 14ins:36cm. No mark

A large pair of ironstone jars, the deep blue bodies enamelled and gilt with butterflies and foliage. Although unmarked this form is well known.

£300 — £400

G.M. & C.J. Mason c.1825-1835
Length 13¼ins:33.7cm
Printed crown and name

A rare Masons patent ironstone inkstand, brightly enamelled and gilt on a blue ground. Most sets of the period have lost one or both pots or covers and can be found from £50 for the dish alone.

£200 — £300

Davenport c.1830
Length 9ins:22.8cm. Printed name

An uncommon object at this date, bourdaloues having gone out of general use in the 1790s. Their purpose and history is perhaps worth repeating here. During the 18th century a preacher by the name of Père Bourdeloue became so popular at the court of Versailles that his church tended to fill up hours before the service was to begin. This, combined with the length of the sermon, obliged ladies to carry suitable emergency equipment to avoid losing their places. By extension the article took the preacher's name. It was, of course, quite acceptable to relieve oneself in church and, indeed, at the dinner table, hence the small cupboards in the sideboards of the time. It is worth remembering that Versailles was built with no lavatories at all. Examples as late as this were made for carriage, and later, rail use.

£30 — £50

Staffordshire
Second quarter of the 19th century
Height 7¾ins:19.8cm. No mark

A blue jasper-dip ice pail with white relief hunting scenes. A well produced piece but not expensive for two reasons, firstly, it is not Wedgwood which it gives the impression of pretending to be and secondly, ice pails have a functional appearance about them which, like Stilton dishes and jardinières, makes them unpopular. A pair, however, appears decorative, £80 — £150.

£35 — £45

Staffordshire c.1830
Height 3¼ins:8.3cm. No mark

A silver lustred sugar bowl, based on a silver shape of about 1775, moulded with flutes and bead borders. The slight scratching does not detract from the price since it might be some guide to the genuineness of the piece. I am very suspicious of much copper and silver lustre supposedly dating from the first quarter of the 19th century.

£7 — £10

Staffordshire c.1830
Height 2½ins:6.4cm. No mark
A silver lustred salt, based on a silver shape of
c.1790.

£6 — £8

Staffordshire c.1835
Height 5ins:12.8cm. No mark
An amusing miniature chamber pot, printed in black and of
appeal to collectors of children's pottery. Items which bear
names can be unpredictable at auction as two bidders
desperate for a piece with a suitable name to give as a present
can push prices to extraordinary levels. As with car licence
plates, the more common the initials or name, the more likely
a high price becomes.

£25 — £35

Staffordshire c.1835
Height 2ins:5cm. No mark
A dual purpose eggcup which would take a hen's egg one way up and a duck or goose (just) the other.
It could also be used as a napkin ring. Crisply cast in buff stoneware and sprigged with white scrolling
leaves.

£5 — £10 each

Possibly Fulham
c.1840
Length 11ins:27.9cm
Impressed retailer's mark
A saltglazed stoneware spirit flask of large size. Although not marked by the maker the more common retailer's marks are a reliable guide to dating. A check with the Trades Directories will indicate when a particular trader was at a certain address. This example bore the mark "T. Balance, Wine and Brandy Merchant, Red Lion, 197 Ratcliff Highway".

£80 — £120

Stephen Green c.1840
Length 8½ins:21.6cm. Impressed name
A spirit flask in the form of a flint lock pistol, the saltglazed stoneware of almost chocolate-brown colour. This form of pistol was in fact in favour c.1800.

£35 — £45

Samuel Alcock and Co. c.1840
Height 12ins:30.5cm. Impressed Alcock and crown
Two earthenware drug jugs of good quality, painted in claret and gilding on a lemon ground. Having been out of favour for a long period, drug jars are beginning to show some rise in price as they are quite decorative kitchen objects.

£50 — £70

Possibly Scottish mid-19th century
Diameter 3¼ins:8.2cm. No mark

A very rare example of an uncommon object — an earthenware carpet bowl. Made for use down the long corridors of Scottish country houses and castles, they can be found in a variety of patterns. A set comprises thirteen balls; a small jack and four sets of three balls identified by colour. A reasonably well decorated piece in good condition (they are often damaged in play), about £8 — £10; set, £200 — £250.
£25 — £35

Staffordshire mid-19th century
Ewer 13ins:33cm. No mark

An earthenware ewer and basin muzzily transfer printed in blue with lovers at a cottage gate. Typical of thousands of washing sets which would have been found in houses throughout the country in the middle of the century, and which have survived in fair numbers. One would expect some upward movement in price in the near future. No longer of much use except perhaps for floral displays, they look well with pine furniture and have a strong market in the United States.
£15 — £20

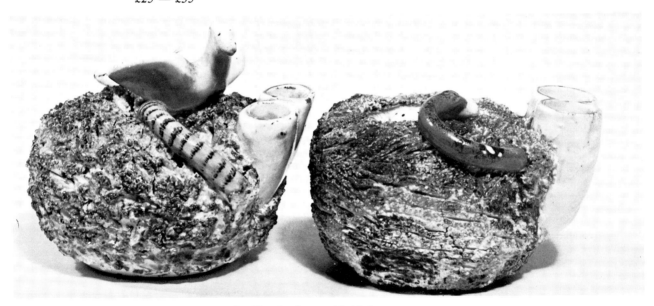

Staffordshire mid-19th century
Height 3¾ins:9.5cm. No mark

An absurd pair of pottery ink-well and pen holders in the form of birds' nests attacked by a snake. Crudely potted and coloured, these have little to recommend them and the one on the right has the bird broken off, but they are typical of large quantities of Staffordshire wares produced throughout the 19th century.
£10 — £12

A Bristol pottery spirit barrel brightly painted by William Fifield with flowers and the initials J.C., 1810-15. 5½ins:14cm. £80 — £120.

A Doulton Burslem earthenware clockcase, c.1890. 8¼ins:21cm. Printed name. £120 — £150.

A Robert Heron Wemyss pottery inkstandish hand painted, c.1880. 10¼ins:26cm. Impressed R.H. and S and printed T. Goode. In crazed condition lacking wells, £70 — £100; in good condition, £150 — £250.

Staffordshire mid-19th century
Height 9½ins:22.8cm. Impressed F28
A chamber pot with risqué print and message, the lettering of unusually high standard.

£25 — £35

Possibly Pratt c.1850
Height 5½ins:14cm. No mark
A redware jar and cover, transfer printed in black, and hand painted in bright enamels with a scene of eastern inspiration. Of far better quality than the contemporary vase on p.192 but using the same idea of a black outline hand coloured.

£8 — £12

Probably F. & R. Pratt & Co. c.1850
Height 11½ins:29.3cm. No mark
A rare clockcase, the green body transfer printed with a vaguely Babylonian scene of warriors. Although rare, such oddities are not in demand, particularly if they lack a working movement.

£40 — £60

Staffordshire c.1850
Height 8¾ins:22.4cm. No mark
A spill holder in the form of a brown hollow stump, hung with a coloured satchel and game. This piece with flaking enamel. Good example, £10 — £12. Good pair. £25 — £35.

£8 — £10

Glasgow
Fern Lane Pottery 1856
Height 14ins:35.6cm
Incised name
A salt-glazed stoneware salt kiln and cover bearing an impressed date at the mouth. An unusual object with more of the feel of the 17th or early 18th century. The flanking figures are those of Tam o'Shanter and Souter Johnny. The factory is not recorded in Godden and this piece may have been a special commission.

£120 — £180

Minton 1864
Length 12½ins:31.8cm
Impressed name and date code
A clear glazed game pie dish, which can be found in majolica colouring, £150 — £250.

£20 — £30

99

Minton 1865
Diameter 7ins:17.5cm
Impressed name and date code

The exact function of these two shallow dishes is not known. The sides with moulded and coloured strawberries, the interior and base turquoise. They must either be wine coasters or cache-pot stands but in either case the decoration seems inappropriate. Not of much interest.

£15 — £20

Probably George Jones c.1870
Height 9½ins:24.1cm
Moulded registration of design

A well moulded and very clearly and brightly coloured majolica camel sweetmeat, the turquoise saddle packs hollow. The underside of the base glazed in well defined green, and brown 'tortoiseshell' which this factory seems to have controlled better than Wedgwood or Minton. The registration mark is too blurred for an exact dating but apparently from the first cycle ending before 1868. The presence of a definite attribution or mark would add considerably to the value.

£200 — £350

Minton 1870
Height 18¾ins:47.5cm
Impressed name and date code

An attractive garden seat closely based on a Chinese original, the sides and top perced with *cash* (cash being the Chinese for money, hence our word) and transfer printed in blue with scrolling lotus. Pair £250 — £350.

£100 — £150

Minton 1870-1877
Length 6¾ins:17.2cm. Inlaid name
A good salt in cream coloured earthenware inlaid, by Charles Toft, with buff and ochre clays after a 16th century inspired design. Toft exhibited several items in the 1862 London International Exhibition which were engraved for the Art Union catalogues. The technique was named by Minton 'Henri Deux' ware since it was based on wares produced at St. Porchaire in the reign of Henry II of France. Some of the pieces which include vases and tazze are close copies, others use the technique on derivative forms. Prices range from about £60 up to a possible £1,000 for a major exhibition piece.
£150 — £200

Probably George Jones 1872
Diameter 15ins:38.3cm
Impressed registration and painted pattern number
An attractive and usable flower bowl, moulded and well coloured. Cracked example. £30 — £40.
£50 — £80

Minton 1875
Height 18¼ins:46.4cm. Impressed name and date code
A majolica seat with heavily moulded and brightly coloured stylised foliage.
£120 — £180

W.T. Copeland 1875
Height 24½ins:62.3cm
Impressed name and date code
A pair of pedestals moulded with white figures on a blue ground, the floral swags coloured. Probably made originally for specific jardinières which have now parted company; with these, £500 — £600; single stand, £60 — £80.
£200 — £250

Probably George Jones c.1880
Length 23½ins:59.7cm. Impressed registration
A fish dish with cover and strainer. The cover well moulded and coloured, with a salmon resting on a bed of leaves. Despite its high quality, the large size is a factor limiting its appeal.
£220 — £250

Minton c.1879
Height 11¾ins:30cm
Impressed name and date code
An interesting majolica centrepiece, the shell moulded dishes below a putto blacksmith representing Industry. The whole well modelled after Hughues Protat, see p.83.
£70 — £100

George Jones c.1880
Height 6¾ins:17cm. No mark

A majolica box and cover moulded with shells on the cover and seaweed on the sides, the whole brightly enamelled. It was presumably made for some fish contents, sardines or paste perhaps. The designer has not considered the fragility of the earthenware body and has allowed too many sharp edges and corners making it unlikely to survive intact. Example with a few chips, £40 — £60.

£70 — £100

Staffordshire c.1880
Height 6ins:15cm. No mark

A miniature earthenware lavatory bowl carried by a commercial traveller as a sample of his company's wares. This particular example turned up in Florence and was very probably taken there by a hopeful salesman intent on converting the Italians to the joys of English plumbing. Usable examples well transfer printed in blue and extracted whole from renovated houses are now finding a ready market, the better specimens fetching up to £80. The main problem is the cost of conversion to modern plumbing if used for their original purpose; many are used as jardinières.

£30 — £50

George Jones c.1880
Height 18½ins:47cm. Impressed monogram

A very decorative Japanese taste garden seat with moulded cranes on a blue ground amongst coloured lotus, the top simulating matting. This example poorly coloured and moulded. Good example. £200 — £300.

£150 — £180

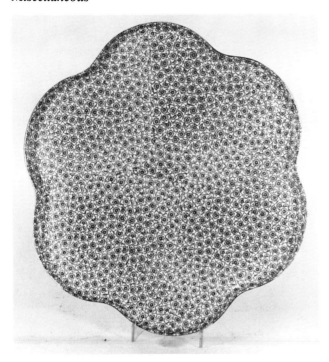

Royal Worcester 1881
Diameter 24½ins:61.5cm
Printed crowned circle, date code
and registration of design
A very large 'lazy Susan' printed in underglaze blue with prunus flowers supported on a revolving wood stand. An uncommon and decorative piece but somewhat too large, a 15ins. (38cm) example would be more manageable, £30 — £40.

£25 — £35

Mintons c.1885
Height 18½ins:47cm. Impressed name
A later development of the straight copy on p.100, moulded with studs and printed in browns and yellows. Although more interesting from a design point of view, less obvious to the interior designer, and, since he dictates the price of these seats, less expensive. Originally made for orangeries and conservatories in country houses, they are now serving as side tables.

£100 — £150

Mintons 1887
Height 19ins:48.2cm. Impressed Mintons and date code
A majolica garden seat of unusually bizarre form, well moulded and brightly coloured. Its main drawback is that of being seen only to advantage from the position as photographed; when viewed from above, as it normally would be, the monkey is lost under the pad seat.

£250 — £350

G.L. Ashworth & Bros. late 19th century
Diameter 10½ins:26.7cm
Printed Masons Ironstone ribbon mark

A chamber pot transfer printed in blue and brightly coloured from an early 19th century design. The shape has also been taken from an earlier original. Despite the Masons mark, it is a later product from the Ashworth factory. The washing bowl from the same set, £40 — £60; the jug, £35 — £45.

£25 — £35

Mintons late 19th century
Chamber diameter 9ins:22.8cm
Printed globe mark and title 'Taymouth'

Part of a toilet set comprising two chamber pots, two soap dishes, liners and covers, jug and basin and slop pail, all with printed, coloured and gilt flowers. Somewhat dreary in appearance and not popular objects. Odd pieces from £5.

£60 — £80

Derbyshire late 19th century
Height 18ins:45.7cm. No mark

This strange earthenware tower is in fact a Bargeman's companion and is in several pieces, each with floral motifs on a treacle ground. It forms a spittoon, tobacco jar and weight, goblet and candlestick. Along with the barge teapots (see pp.186, 187) coming to be appreciated for their rustic charm.

£40 — £60

Burmantofts late 19th century
Height 24¾ins:63cm
Impressed name

A boringly designed umbrella stand, the cast decoration under a lime green glaze shading to blue green at the base. Burmantofts was a short-lived venture that produced a few good art pottery vases usually under green, blue or brown glazes.

£20 — £30

Sunderland/Staffordshire late 19th century
Diameter 12½ins:31.5cm. No mark

A two-handled earthenware chamber pot transfer printed in sepia naïvely coloured with a view of the Clifton Suspension Bridge. The interior has a cartoon inscribed "One at a Time Please", the base another, "Now I'm a Grandfather". A good example of the long survival of a popular print. One might think that it could be dated to the middle of the century but the 'japonais' flowers on the sides belie this; they must post-date 1885. Chamber pots are not popular as the soft pottery is often crazed and has absorbed a certain amount of the original contents which is impossible to remove. They are much used in the USA as jardinières.

£20 — £30

Robert Heron & Sons c.1900
Height 7ins:17.8cm. No mark

A Wemyss stylised goose flower holder with brightly coloured plumage, the base with the printed retailer's name of Thomas Goode & Co.

£50 — £70

Robert Heron c.1900
Diameter 12ins:30.5cm
Impressed Wemyss and initials

A Wemyss earthenware basket typically painted with bold pink cabbage roses beneath a turquoise rope twist handle. Wemyss has a small but dedicated following, particulary from the ballet and theatrical profession.
£40 — £60

A. Fenton & Sons c.1900
Height 5¾ins:14.6cm. Printed name

A transfer printed biscuit barrel in blue, touched with speckled gilding on a gilt floral ground. An object of poor quality. The silver-plated mount and cover conforming.

£6 — £8

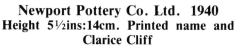

Carlton Ware Ltd. 1920s
Length 5¼ins:13.4cm. Printed circular mark
A Carltonware interpretation of Wedgwood fairyland with Oriental figures in bright lustres and gilding. Very much less interesting than Daisy Makeig-Jones' Wedgwood designs, but nevertheless underpriced at present.

£10 — £15

Royal Doulton early 20th century
Height 10ins:23.3cm
Impressed lion and crowned circle
A stoneware spirit flask made for Dewars and cast after a design by Dudley Hardy with his impressed signature and with humorous Scottish figures. Not a very desirable item for the ceramic collector, but rising in price because of the fast growing interest in bottles.

£20 — £30

Newport Pottery Co. Ltd. 1940
Height 5½ins:14cm. Printed name and Clarice Cliff
A sugar dredger of truly bizarre conception, the rocket form body rising from flower heads and glazed in virulent orange, red, green and yellow. Clarice Cliff has a certain following, some of the designs being sufficiently "art deco" in feel to appeal to collectors of the period.

£25 — £40

Plaques and Tiles

Most plaques used by ceramic artists as a canvas were produced in porcelain as a finer surface could be achieved, but both Minton and more especially, Copeland did make suitable blanks in earthenware. One advantage of earthenware was that it could be made in far larger sizes. Few plaques are marked and attributions are usually based on the knowledge of which artists worked for which factory at a particular time. Copeland, however, seem to have been stricter about marking than most. William Yale, who worked for Copeland, had a vast output and his quality varies from dreadful to very good, his oil-like technique was well adapted to painting on earthenware slabs although some are marred by firing faults. The earthenware tile, which had such an enormous impact on the architecture and even the health of the nation, is perhaps one of the most lasting memorials to Victorian mass-production. Best suited of all wares to the machine, they poured off the production line and onto porches, paths, kitchens, bathrooms, creameries and factories where they lasted, unchanged until the houses were condemned as slums or "improved" and the factories failed to meet new regulations. Fortunately so many were made that they can still be seen *in situ* in back streets all over Britain and a growing number of enthusiasts are collecting them. It would be impossible to illustrate even a minute proportion of the thousands of designs but a few representative examples have been included.

Staffordshire early 19th century
Width 11¼ins:28.5cm. No mark
A very curious plaque which might once have been a teapot stand since there are traces of ball feet at the corners. The naïve gilt silhouette animals on a brown ground are typical of the first quarter of the 19th century. Out of the scope of most collectors and therefore relatively cheap.

£20 — £30

Staffordshire c.1832
Height 8ins:20.3cm. No mark
Dr. Adam Clarke was a famous Wesleyan minister and writer who died in 1832 and this black bordered print probably commemorates the event.

£15 — £30

Moore and Co., Sunderland c.1840
8¼ins. x 9½ins:20.9cm x 24.1cm. Impressed Moore

A plaque with a transfer print of figures in a pseudo-classical landscape by a lake, the border in pink splashed lustre. Landscape plaques are less common than the Iron Bridge, shipping or religious subjects but, as they are invariably imaginary, they are not much in demand. The most interesting point about this plaque is that it has an impressed mark.

£20 — £30

Sunderland c.1840
Width 7ins:18cm. No mark

A black print, hand coloured within a pink-splashed lustre border with brown edge. An exception to the general rule that objects with religious connections generate little interest. Plaques of this type are now so amusing to modern eyes that they find a ready market.

£15 — £20

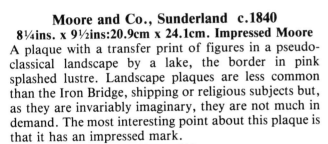

Minton mid-19th century to 1880
6ins:15.4cm square. Impressed Minton and Co.

A heavy encaustic tile formed of a sandwich of different clays in terracotta, yellow, two greens, chocolate and blue, and impressed with a stylised primrose. An attractive and rich result. These encaustic tiles are hard to find without chipped edges.

£5 — £10

**Dixon Phillips
and Co.
and unknown
Mid-19th century
7¼ins. and 6½ins.
18.3cm and 16.5cm
Impressed name
No mark**

Two variations on a theme, the thin earthenware disc with raised rim. The one on the right unusually moulded with angels' heads. The message printed in black.

*£25 — £35
and £30 — £40*

**Sunderland c.1850
8¼ins. x 9½ins:20.9cm x 24.1cm. No mark**

A plaque transfer printed in black with a galleon and a verse "For Peace and Plenty", the rim brown. There is every chance that these plaques were made over a long period, conceivably into the 20th century and dating is usually difficult. Were it easier, a stronger market could well result.

£15 — £25

**W.T. Copeland c.1860
Width 9ins:22.8cm
Impressed crown and name**

A pair of earthenware tiles painted with river scenes, probably by Daniel Lucas, junior. One titled on the reverse "St. Denis and Verion after Turner." A signature would raise the price to £350 — £400. Copeland was one factory that was fairly strict about marking its plaques and tiles although many were probably sold to be decorated outside.

£250 — £350

Staffordshire 1862
12ins. x 18ins.
30.5cm x 45.7cm
No mark
A large plaque painted in William Yale's easily recognisable and rather amateur style, the reverse inscribed "W. Yale, Stoke on Trent" and the title.
£140 — £160

W.T. Copeland c.1870
Diameter 21½ins:54.5cm
Impressed name
A large plaque painted by W. Yale, signed, with a scene of blackberry picking. Far better painted than most of his plaques, compare with the previous example. Pair, £350 — £500. It would have fetched more had it not been circular.
£150 — £200

Minton c.1870
15¼ins. x 11ins:38.8cm. x 28cm. No mark
A good majolica plaque, moulded and coloured with a Renaissance design. The black cartouches were probably originally intended to be filled with a name in gilding. Marked example, £120 — £180.
£150 — £200

Sunderland c.1870
9¼ins:23.4cm. No mark
A plaque with pink and copper splashed lustre border enclosing a black print of the Great Eastern. This ship, built by Isambard Kingdom Brunel, was launched amidst much public interest between November 1857 and January 1858, hampered by numerous accidents and problems. It seems likely that these commemorative plaques were made for a considerable period after the event.
£60 — £80

Minton c.1870
15¾ins. x 36¼ins:40cm x 92cm. No mark
A superbly painted large plaque of Aurora after Guido Reni, signed by Thomas Kirkby. Kirkby was one of Minton's best painters, specialising in figure subjects on earthenware. Despite his importance and the decorative qualities of these plaques they remain surprisingly low in price.
£300 — £500

Mintons 1875
Diameter 15¼ins:38cm. Impressed name, date code
One of a pair of wall plates painted and signed by John Bishop Evans, who worked at Mintons from 1865-85. Well painted but unexciting. The earthenware body lends itself to more vigorous treatment and Evans was far better on the whiter, cleaner porcelain body.
£70 — £100 (pair)

Mintons 1877
12½ins. x 8½ins:31.8cm x 21.6cm
Impressed Minton
An earthenware plaque painted by E. Broughton and dated 1877. A somewhat mawkish subject but the bare-footed girl and the appealing-eyed dog make this an expensive plaque.
£200 — £250

Mintons c.1880
16ins:15.4cm square. Moulded name
A pseudo-mosaic tile with stencilled design in black, blue, terracotta and two shades of grey. An extraordinarily complex production to no great effect, a whole floor would look suspiciously like linoleum, but attractive close to.
£2 — £3

Staffordshire c.1880
6ins. x 12ins:15cm. x 30.5cm. No mark

A pair of earthenware plaques well painted on the olive ground with lions and wolves. Certainly executed by someone with knowledge of ceramic painting but unattributed.

£80 — £120

Minton c.1880
6ins:15.2cm square. Relief name
One of a set of twelve designs after J. Moyr-Smith for Tennyson's "Morte d'Arthur", Transfer printed in grey, brown and black. Complete set, £50 — £80. He designed other tiles including sets of Aesop's Fables and scenes from Shakespeare, his name or initials usually discernible somewhere in the picture, similar prices.

£3 — £5

Mintons 1882
Diameter 11ins:27.9cm. Impressed name and date code
An "out of period" portrait of the young Duke of Wellington, probably painted by a skilled amateur from a print on a factory "blank". Not of interest to commemorative collectors.

£12 — £15

A Yorkshire pottery plaque moulded and painted, c.1800. 9¾ins:24.8cm. £40 — £60.

Sherwin and Cotton c.1890
12ins. x 6ins:30.5cm. x 15cm
Impressed name
Numerous tiles of this type, with various intaglio designs of wild life, politicians and genre subjects, were produced by this factory, some having photographic-style reliefs and moulding as a basis for their production. The glazes vary in thickness to produce the required subtlety of tone although the colours chosen are generally unsubtle in themselves, sepia, green and blue being the most common. They are frequently crazed.

£1 — £4

Mintons 1898
12¼ins. x 6ins:31cm x 16cm. Impressed Mintons and date code

A good earthenware plaque signed by Leon V. Solon. This plaque in art nouveau style was produced by a variety of techniques including slip trailing, used for outlining, the clay squeezed like toothpaste from a bag; raised gilding and brightly coloured slip and glazes. L.V. Solon was the son of Marc Louis Solon, the Minton pâte-sur-pâte artist and studio director, and he soon gained a reputation as great, if not greater, than that of his father, his work being illustrated in *The Studio* and other contemporary journals. He also designed titles for mass-production, £10 upwards. In his turn he also became Art Director of Mintons.

£300 — £500

Staffordshire c.1895-1900
Square 6ins:15.4cm
Indecypherable moulded registration
A very attractive and brightly coloured tile in two blues
and shaded greens with painted orange stamens on
cream, apparently slip trailed and glazed but actually
moulded to simulate slip trailing.
£4 — £6

James Hadley and Sons c.1900
Diameter 12ins:30.5cm
Impressed Hadley's Fine Art Terracotta
A rare terracotta plaque with a relief of a Kate
Greenaway-type girl within coloured slip borders,
modelled by James Hadley, the Royal Worcester
designer, who set up on his own in 1896. Although
uncommon, these plaques are relatively inexpensive
because they are not from the Royal Worcester factory,
even though made by the factory's most famous
sculptor. The material is soft and prone to rubbing.
£200 — £300

Royal Doulton c.1910
9¾ins:24.8cm. Printed trade mark
Plaque printed and painted in blue, although the printed
lines are not readily distinguishable, with a sketchy
figure subject. The two flaws at the bottom are firing
faults. Pair, £100 — £150.
£40 — £60

Plates and Dishes

With the exception of a very few hand-painted plates and some Royal Doulton transfer printed and hand-coloured specimens, almost everything in this section has been part of a service. Even the majolica dishes were not sold as singles but were originally dessert or sea food sets. There is a growing market of "specimens", transfer printed underglaze blue plates from the first forty years of the nineteenth century. There were dozens of small factories in Staffordshire at the beginning of the century producing these wares for export to the United States of America, appropriately decorated with American views. These form a flourishing market and single plates can fetch up to £500. There is a comparable, but less financially demanding interest in this country, with collectors searching out local views. Several books have appeared on the market recently which help to attribute the prints to particular factories, but it must be remembered that much copying went on. Another area receiving attention is the children's wares which were produced throughout the century; these often have a great deal of charm and reflect the occasionally odd attitude to children of the time. Most of these sell for £2 — £30 but very many of the most expensive commemorative pieces were made for children, witness the wares made for Queen Victoria's Coronation.

There is a booming market in Royal Doulton plates (p.131) as indeed for Doulton moulded jugs; plates and dishes which retain their interest mainly as services should be sought in the next section, Services.

Joshua Heath
Early 19th century
Diameter 9½ins:24.2cm. No mark
A crudely underglaze-blue, transfer printed, earthenware plate, with a sub-oriental pattern. The design probably close to 1800, although it could well have been used any time during the first twenty years of the century. Early plates such as this tend to be very light, thinly potted, with a glaze tending towards blue, especially noticeable where it has collected thickly. The printing is generally in a very dark blue and examples are rarely marked. Compare the border with the commemorative plate on p.28.
£5 — £8

Spode c.1812
Width 16ins:40.6cm
Impressed and printed name
A large and decorative meat dish printed in underglaze-blue with the Tiber pattern. Not one of the rarest patterns but effective in the larger sizes. Plates, from £5.
£40 — £60

Josiah Spode c.1820
Width 16½ins:41.9cm. Printed and impressed name
A good underglaze-blue transfer printed "Indian Sporting Pattern" meat dish, titled on the reverse "Driving a Bear out of Sugar Canes". An amusingly rural English landscape bizarrely populated with bears, elephants and mounted British, the foreground with miniature volcanoes that are probably anthills. This particular series of Indian scenes are now much sought after. Plates, £20 — £30.
£100 — £150

G.M. and C.J. Mason c.1820
Width 14½ins:36.2cm
Impressed "Patent" mark
An unusual ironstone fruit stand, decorated with brightly enamelled Imari patterns and with good gilding. Mason designs at this date were frequently of surprising complexity and technical competence. There is a devoted band of Mason followers, keen to buy good examples.
£80 — £120

121

John Rogers and Son c.1825
Width 19ins:48.2cm. Impressed name
A large meat dish, transfer printed in blue
with the unlikely combination of a Chinese
figure on a zebra in what might pass as Kew
Gardens, all within a border of English
flowers. The clear printing and ridiculous
subject matter make this a highly desirable
piece.

£40 — £60

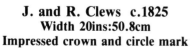

Ralph Stevenson and Williams c.1825
Diameter 10ins:25.5cm. Printed names
An interesting plate, transfer printed in blue, with a clear
print of the Waterworks, Philadelphia, USA, and therefore
of American interest. The covered waggon as used by the
settlers who opened up the West adds to its desirability,
although it is somewhat out of place in a very English-
looking and civilised country park setting. The factory was
very short lived and seems to have concentrated on export
wares.

£100 — £150

J. and R. Clews c.1825
Width 20ins:50.8cm
Impressed crown and circle mark
A large meat dish transfer printed in pale blue with a
view named on the reverse of "A Picturesque View of
Newburg, Hudson River". Although of American
interest, it would fetch much the same in this country
where such pieces are rarer, since they were made for
export and have not made the journey back across the
Atlantic. Dinner plate, £20 — £30.

£80 — £120

Dillwyn, Swansea 1825-1840
Diameter 6¼ins:15.8cm. Impressed names

A black printed plate within a moulded floral border made only slightly more interesting by the impressed Swansea mark. Without mark, £25 — £35.

£35 — £45

Staffordshire c.1830
Diameter 10ins:25.5cm. No mark

A plate printed with a view of the Dam and Waterworks, Philadelphia including a paddle steamer. An American export piece but fetching the same sort of price in this country.

£70 — £100

Enoch Wood and Sons c.1830
Diameter 10ins:25.5cm. Impressed name and eagle

A classic plate combining all that is needed to generate a high price. It is well printed in dark blue with an early steam locomotive within a shell border and is titled on the reverse "The Baltimore and Ohio Railroad". Enoch Wood supplied many American market services which usually bear the eagle as part of the mark and are usually titled. The presence of this shell border is also a warning sign that the piece may be of American interest even if untitled.

£180 — £200

Staffordshire c.1830
Width 12½ins:31.8cm. No mark

A rare and desirable dish printed in underglaze blue with a paddle steamer on the Ohio river at Louisville, Kentucky, passing buildings on the shore, within a flower border.

£350 — £400

Staffordshire c.1830
Diameter 6⅝ins:16.8cm. No mark
A brightly coloured child's plate in iron red, lime green and yellow over a black print of an improving nature, the rim moulded with flowers. This piece is cracked. A good example, £8 — £10.

£3 — £5

John Rogers and Son c.1830
Width 19ins:48.3cm. Impressed name
A large meat dish in blue, with a romanticised Chinese/Indian landscape including an elephant with its **mahout.**

£40 — £60

Staffordshire c.1830
Width 10¾ins:27.3cm. No mark
A rare and attractive blue and white transfer printed basket with a bear hunting scene. Commoner in the United States of America where most were sent for export, but still fetching a similar price in England. This example has a slight crack in rim. In good condition, £180 — £220.

£150 — £180

Copeland and Garret 1833-1847
Diameter 9½ins:24.1cm. Printed name
A well printed plate in bitter chocolate brown with a Continental scene. These scenes were popular at this period due to the interest in "the Grand Tour". Perhaps on this return, the traveller bought a new service to remind him of his travels, rediscovering the Lago di Como under a sea of gravy. Plates rise to £5 — £10 in a serice; tureens, £30 — £100; meat plates, £10 — £30; vegetable dishes, £30 — £50.

£2 — £3

Possibly F. & R. Pratt c.1835
Width 19ins:48cm. No mark

A large blue and white venison dish, moulded with gravy runnels leading to a well at one end. The large central castle scene is surrounded by other country houses and flowers. The price of large meat dishes is very much dependent upon their attractiveness and the scenes depicted. Identifiable views are at a premium.

£50 — £70

Staffordshire c.1840
Diameter 9¾ins:24.8cm. Imressed S

A plate of pleasing simplicity, transfer printed in green with the equestrian statue of William III, Prince of Orange, and probably made for the Irish market.

£18 — £22

Staffordshire c.1840
Diameter 10¾ins:27.4cm. No mark

A dinner plate transfer printed in brown, with Europeans trading in a Chinese port, probably intended as Canton, and titled on the reverse "Commerce". Interesting only for its idealised impression of the Far East.

£2 — £3

Charles James Mason & Co. c.1840
Width 20¼ins:51.4cm. Printed crown and initials

A meat dish, transfer printed in green, with a central scene of Napoleon at the Battle of Marengo.

£25 — £30

Staffordshire mid-19th century
Diameter 7½ins:19.1cm. No mark

A child's pottery plate, moulded with the alphabet at the rim, and with a black transfer print of a passenger train in the centre. Collectable by both railway and children's ware enthusiasts.

£30 — £40

William Smith and Co. c.1850
Diameter 6½ins:16.5cm. Impressed initials

A child's plate transfer printed in brown, with a scene of Paul and Virginia within a flower moulded border. Unmarked example, £2 — £3.

£8 — £10

Possibly Copeland mid-19th century
Diameter 11¼ins:28.5cm. No mark

A deep plate, boldly painted in bright blue, red and green stylised flowers with fuchsias in the centre. The florets have been stamped, possibly from a potato block, in purple. Probably because of its bright and direct colouration, large quantities of these dishes, many of large size, can be found in India, some of which are marked Copeland and date from as late as the 1880s.

£8 — £10

Staffordshire c.1860
Width 9ins:22.9cm. No mark

An earthenware dessert plate, moulded with strawberries and grapes and coloured in blue, yellow and green on a brown ground. Typical of thousands of similar plates in shops all over the country, more usually with a bottle green glaze, at the same price. They will, no doubt, rise in price quite soon particularly if in complete services, when they already make £5 — £8 per piece if marked. Wedgwood examples are not uncommon but are fetching in the region of £5 — £8.

£2 — £5

W.T. Copeland c.1860
Diameter 14½ins:36.8cm. Impressed name and crown
An interesting plate printed and coloured with a robin
and the legend "A Happy Christmas To You", the
design taken from the *Illustrated London News* of 1858.
Its topicality is a decidedly limiting factor in its appeal.
It would seem in appropriate to have it hanging on a
wall except for the twelve days of Christmas and for
perhaps a few before.
£30 — £40

Minton 1869
Diameter 10⅛ins:25.7cm
Impressed Minton, date code and registration of design
A sepia printed earthenware plate, hand coloured in
subdued monochrome with snipe. The vacuous centre
makes it unsuitable for display but a set of twelve would
be usable, £50 — £80.
£2 — £3

Minton 1869
Diameter 9ins:22.8cm Impressed Minton and date code
A majolica oyster plate, glazed pale green with seaweed
borders. Set of twelve, £160 — £180.
£8 — £10

Left: **Minton**
Right: **Possibly George Jones c.1870. Width 10ins:25.4cm**
Impressed Minton and registration marks
Two nut dishes, similarly designed, with a squirrel forming the handle and seated on overlapping leaves. The one on the left from Minton, the other anonymous, but possibly George Jones. It is interesting to note that both bear a registration of design mark, supposedly giving protection to the design for four years, although one has obviously been inspired by, but not copied, the other.

£60 — £80

George Jones and Sons c.1875
Diameter 9½ins:24.2cm.
Impressed initials and crescent
An uncommon majolica plate, moulded with a girl in pink and green dress, shrimping in a turquoise sea. The wide rim is decorated with aubergine bladder-wrack and brightly coloured shells. Plates with naturalistic moulded figure subjects are rare. This example could have been improved by better colouring of the centre panel, £30 — £40.

£20 — £30

George Jones c.1876
11ins:28cm
Impressed monogram and registration of design
An uncommon dish, attractively moulded and coloured with butterflies and orchids. A good, bold design and very much of the period. George Jones earthenware is at least as good as the generality of Minton.

£50 — £80

William Brownfield 1880
8½ins:21.5cm. Impressed name, title and date code
An aesthetic movement, black transfer print of a peacock and peonies. The designer was trying to be up-to-date with a *Japonais* ho-o (phoenix) among peonies (but the bird has turned into a peacock, in Chinese, not Japanese style) and has confused things further by calling the pattern "Ivory". A neglected period which should show signs of movement in the near future. A dessert service of twelve plates and four stands, £35 — £45.

50p — £1

Mintons 1881
Diameter 11ins:28cm
Impressed Mintons and registration
A good majolica dish, presumably for oysters, the yellow and grey fish amongst green and purple seaweed around a blue well. A successful design, amusing and evocative of the period. Pair, £100 — £150. A set of twelve would not, in this case, fetch a premium over the cost of six pairs.

£40 — £60

Royal Worcester 1881
Diameter 12ins:30.5cm. Printed mark and date code
A pair of large plates, incised and black filled by Albert Binns (son of R.W. Binns) who died at the age of twenty. Although uncommon, they are outside the general run of Worcester collectors.
£100 — £150

Staffordshire probably 1887
Diameter 7½ins:19cm. Impressed numerals

A child's plate of a supposedly educative nature, although any child with an inquiring mind might ask awkward questions about the wine, women and vice mentioned in the black transfer print which might have caused more trouble than a blank plate. The rim is moulded with flowers and painted with pink line border. Dr. Franklin's appalling Maxims abound and would make an amusing collection. The reverse bears what appears to be a fractional date code $^3/_{87}$ showing for how long these plates were popular after they first appeared in the 1830s.

£5 — £8

Spode (W.T. Copeland) c.1900
Diameter 10ins:25.4cm
Printed mark in green and 'Kings'

An unusual dinner plate, transfer printed in underglaze blue and painted in iron red and gilding with an "imari" pattern, this exclusive to the King's Regiment, as it has been since its introduction in the 1820s. Early specimen, £10 — £15. Theoretically a reasonably complete service would be unobtainable, but the Regiment did sell over 300 pieces of mixed periods at Sotheby's Belgravia in 1971 for £430; it would now fetch £2,500 — £3,500, such has been the rise in usable services.

£5 — £8

Booths early 20th century
9ins:22.9cm. Printed name and crown

If you cannot afford the first period Worcester, originally painted by James Giles, at about £500, then Booths produced these attractive and fairly accurate copies in pottery complete with blue scale ground, transfer printed coloured birds and gilding. The example shown has crazed and stained brown, a fault with the thinly potted body. Good example, £3 — £5, dessert service of twelve plates and four shaped dishes, £80 — £120.

£2 — £3

Royal Doulton c.1920
Diameter 9ins:23cm. Printed lion, crown and circle
A plate printed in black and hand coloured with a scene from Robin Hood. Numerous others on this and other rural subjects were produced. There is a strong American following which is tending to raise the prices quite quickly.

£8 — £12

Wemyss c.1920
Width 7ins:17.8cm. Impressed and painted Wemyss
A small tray from a dressing table set, boldly painted with pink cabbage roses and green leaves.

£18 — £22

Royal Doulton c.1920s
Diameter 10¼ins:26.1cm. Printed crowned circle
An earthenware plate, Doulton's answer to Wedgwood Fairyland lustre. Printed Doulton wares of this period are rising in price.

£15 — £20

Royal Doulton c.1925
Diameter 10½ins:26.6cm
Printed lion, crown and circle
A large plate printed in black and coloured, typical of a number of similar plates issued by Doulton's with different "portraits". Others include "The Bookworm", "The Jester", "The Mayor" and "The Squire", all at the same price.

£10 — £12

Services

Earthenware became respectable for the gentry to eat from with the introduction in about 1765 of Josiah Wedgwood's Queensware. Capable of fine potting and decoration, it had one great drawback — its fragility. Early on in the nineteenth century Charles James Mason developed ironstone china which had advantages over both pottery and porcelain, not the least of which was its strength, particularly important today for those who buy them to use. It is a tribute to the original potters that the enamels and even the gilding will suffer the indignities of modern detergents and the washing-up machine without complaint. In contradiction to the usual business of bulk buying, the price of single items *rises* rather than falls when in a service, thus a single plate might fetch 50p — £1, and a tureen and cover £60 — £80, becoming £5 — £10 and £150 — £200 in a usable quantity.

Dessert services are no longer used for the purpose for which they were originally intended and their value, when separated from a dinner service, depends directly on their decorativeness, unless by a particularly desirable manufacturer, Spode or Mason for example.

Underglaze transfer printed services were produced in vast quantities much of it for export, particularly to the United States of America, at the beginning of the century, not only in the common blue but also in brown, black and green. These rarely appear in large enough quantities for use nowadays, presumably because the cheaper earthenware was made for a less genteel class who did not entertain in large numbers. Apart from size, the other factors that dictate price are the same as those that govern any other field: condition, attractiveness, quality, and the factory (this last normally the most important, but in this section the least).

Children's services or "toys" are much sought after if of good quality and of early date.

Davenport c.1805
Height 5ins:12.8cm. Impressed name
An earthenware sauce tureen on fixed stand, transfer printed in red with a country house and garden. Complete with cover, £40 — £60; pair complete, £120 — £150.

£30 — £50

Spode first quarter of the 19th century
Impressed Spode
A sauce tureen, cover and stand painted in brown and bright green with stylised currants. Set of further tureen, two baskets, comport, six dishes and eighteen plates. Tureen, cover and stand, £30 — £50; plate, £4 — £5.
£300 — £350 the service

Spode 1805-1815
Impressed and printed name
A "new stone" earthenware service consisting of twelve soup, twelve dessert, and twenty-four dinner plates, soup tureen, cover and stand, two sauce tureens, covers and stands, four vegetable dishes and covers and five meat plates. Each piece printed with a Ch'ien Lung-based "famille rose" design. The service is worth more split into individual items than as a usable service.
£500 — £700 the service

Hicks and Meigh c.1810
Height 14ins:35.6cm
Printed crown and Ironstone. Warranted
A colourful and good quality tureen, cover and stand, the stone china body in underglaze-blue and bright enamels. Plate, £4 — £6. Service of twenty soup, dinner and dessert plates, three various tureens, four vegetable dishes and six meat dishes, £1,200 — £1,800.
£120 — £150

G.M. and C.J. Mason 1815-1820
Impressed and printed marks
including Prince of Wales feathers

A tureen, cover and stand from an ironstone service comprising soup tureen, cover and stand, two tureens, covers and stands, two covered vegetable dishes, four vegetable dishes and fifteen each of soup, dinner and side plates. Each piece transfer printed in black and hand coloured after a Chinese "famille rose" original named by Masons "the table and flower pattern". The Prince of Wales feathers mark is rare. Mason ironstone sells at a premium (compare with the Spode service below).

£1,500 — £2,000 the service

Spode 1815-1830
Spode seal

An Imari pattern service transfer printed in underglaze-blue and hand coloured with bright flowers, comprising two soup tureens, covers and stands, six vegetable dishes and covers, five sauce tureens, covers and stands, fifteen meat dishes in sizes, fifty dinner plates, thirty soup plates and twelve side plates.

£1,200 — £1,500 the service

Spode c.1820
5ins. and 11ins:12.7cm and 27.8cm
Printed or impressed Spode, printed title

Two pickle dishes from the popular Indian Sporting Scenes, the larger with "Hunting a Deer Dog". Items from this series are more expensive than any other mass-produced wares of the period, apart from those of American interest.

£35 — £45 and £10 — £15

Edward and George Phillips 1822-1834
Printed E. & G.P.
A child's tea service printed in blue with a girl and her lamb or flowers and titled on the base "Pett Lamb" (*sic*). Price given for the pieces shown plus two further cups and saucers. A more complete service with six cups and saucers, milk jug and sucrier, £60 — £80.
£20 — £25 the service

William Hackwood 1827-1843
Impressed name
An unusually complete and early transfer printed dolls' service of sixty-five pieces. Particularly interesting for being marked. Dolls' and/or children's services seem to be rising in price faster than the average service.
£150 — £180 the service

Copeland & Garrett 1833-1847
Printed and impressed marks pattern number 5266
Part of an extensive service of 186 pieces which included two soup tureens, cover and stands, four
vegetable dishes, four sauce tureens and sixty-eight dinner plates. The combination of a large number of
pieces making the service very usable, and a quite bright pattern, the "New Fayence", printed and hand-
coloured, determines the high price. Soup tureen, £80 — £120; plate, £1 — £2.
£1,000 — £1,500 the service

Charles Meigh c.1840
Plate 9ins:22.8cm. Printed name and title
Impressed Improved Stone China
A dish and plate from a dreary dessert service,
transfer printed in green and picked out with
yellow dots, titled on the reverse "Privet
Berry". Service of twelve plates, four circular,
two square, two oval dishes and a comport,
£100 — £120.

£3 — £4 each

Charles Meigh & Sons c.1855
Printed initials
Samples from a "Ceylon" pattern service.
The underglaze-blue printed pattern of inky
tone blurred into the glaze and hand
coloured on top. The definition of the blue
pattern and the way the hand colouring
blends with it are most important in
assessing the price. Service of twenty-four
dinner, twelve dessert and side plates, soup
tureen, two sauce tureens both with covers
and stands, six meat dishes in sizes and a
fruit stand, £480 — £500. Odd plates as little
as £1 — £2. Service of similar number of
pieces but with a well integrated design
would cost half as much again.

*A Thomas Fell, Newcastle on Tyne, pearlware comport, hand painted with a bird, c.1820. 13½ins:34.2cm.
Impressed Fell. £80 — £120.*

*A Copeland earthenware tazza and plate, brown printed and hand coloured in early 19th century style. 8ins.
and 8¼ins:20.2cm and 21cm. Impressed Copeland and date code for 1874. £5 — £10 each.*

Thomas Fell and Co. mid-19th century
Impressed name, anchor and crown and coat of arms
A dinner plate and a vegetable dish and cover from a service of approximately ninety pieces including four similar dishes, twelve soup plates and thirty dinner plates, etc. A large and usable service, each piece printed and hand coloured with bold flowers. As modern services have become more expensive over the last few years, the price of second-hand services, often of better quality and frequently cheaper, has also risen.
£180 — £250 the service

G.M. & C.J. Mason c.1845
Impressed name and Real Ironstone China and printed Mason Royal Arms
A plate and sauce tureen from an ironstone service, printed in underglaze-blue and coloured in iron-red and gilding, loosely based on a Chinese original. Soup tureen, £80 — £120; vegetable tureen, cover and stand, £60 — £80; sauce boat, £40 — £60; plates, £4 — £6; meat dishes, £15 — £80.

Royal Worcester 1878
Printed and impressed crowned circle mark and date code
A royal lily pattern service, printed in blue and with brown and gilt rim. Price given for twelve each of soup and dessert plates, twenty-four dinner plates, soup tureen, four vegetable and four sauce tureens, cover and stands, and five meat dishes. Probably ranks amongst the cheapest buys of the period. A quite amusing and usable service, but suffering from the usual problem of how to keep the plates warm without cracking or crazing them.

£200 — £300 the service

Staffordshire c.1883
Printed title and registration of design

An earthenware service printed in brown and picked out in pastel enamels and gilding, titled "Palmyra" on the back. Obviously a popular pattern as it turns up frequently. Price given for twelve each of soup, side and dessert and twenty-four dinner plates, soup tureen, four vegetable dishes and covers, four sauce tureens, covers and stands, six meat dishes and a venison dish.

£120 — £150 the service

Royal Worcester 1887
Printed crowned circle mark and date code

A variation in pattern on the service shown on p.138 but less desirable. Price given for the same quantity.

£120 — £150 the service.

W.T. Copeland 1895
Length 7ins:18cm
Printed name, impressed registration and date code

A sauceboat printed in underglaze-blue with the Tower Pattern introduced in the early 19th century and registered in 1888. The crude pastry-moulded rim is typical of late pieces.

£8 — £10

Booths late 19th century
Printed name

A dinner service decorated with floral panels of no great quality. Booths produced a quantity of usuable table ware around the turn of the century, often in a soft body prone to crazing. Price given for tureen, cover and stand, four vegetable dishes and covers, twelve soup plates, dinner and dessert plates, and five serving dishes. Single plates might be found in junk shops for about 30p.

£100 — £150 the service

Staffordshire Figures

After a great deal of debate, it has been decided to split this section of the book into three parts, Portrait and Titled Figures 1800-1859, Portrait and Titled Figures 1860-1900, and Miscellaneous. Within the Portrait and Titled sections the figures have been assembled chronologically as it seems more important to give some guidance on the dating of figures than to stick to the more usual divisions adopted by books on Staffordshire figures splitting them into collectable categories such as Military, Royalty and so on.

The collector, as with the commemorative collector, must make some decision, unless he has an almost bottomless purse and a warehouse, to limit his acquisitions by applying some sort of scheme. The most usual is to buy only contemporary portrait figures and then to pick on a field of particular interest such as sport or religion. There are usually enough (often fortuitous) variations in any one figure to satisfy the desire for rarity and even the "unique". With a production line that depended to a great extent on the manual dexterity of the artisan, variations in limb position, colouration and titling inevitably occur, but can lead to dramatic price increases.

There is a fine dividing line between the badly modelled, crudely cast and garishly coloured and therefore undesirable, and the badly modelled, crudely cast, garishly coloured and naïve and therefore eminently desirable; a dividing line that can only be drawn by the collector. In the comments that accompany each photograph in any section the reader must make up his own mind whether any apparent criticism is justified. It is possible to find two almost identical figures with different titles; this is an example of the potter being economical with his moulds. When sales dropped for the one, a "new" hero could be produced much more quickly by adapting the old mould. The names can be found applied by several methods, by indenting into the wet clay from printers' type and then painted black or gilded, by painting or gilding in script and capital letters, or by relief moulding which again can be coloured or gilt or left plain. Many were issued un-named with a simple gilt line, and genuine old figures lacking a title have been noted with a fake modern name added.

The Staffordshire portrait field is in the happy position of changing yearly as previously unrecorded figures appear on the market, and the previously unidentified are unambiguously attributed to an event or person from contemporary illustrations, and a number of excellent books have been published over the last few years.

It does not seem to have been generally commented on that the majority of the best early figures are made of porcelain and not pottery. They are modelled "in the round" although the detail at the rear is fairly crude whereas the "flat back" figures have little or no detail on the reverse.

Staffordshire figures were sold cheaply and were a folk market, they were "cheap and cheerful" (which may or may not include the ever popular murder series according to taste) and, because they were part of the everyday life of the working classes, many have suffered damage which the collector will tolerate far more than his counterpart in the porcelain field. Nevertheless, a fine example will fetch a premium over the ordinary; good colouring, casting, and titling as well as condition being important. Restoration can be difficult to spot, but the head is the most obvious part prone to damage, and fakes are appearing on the market (see "Fakes" p.234).

**Staffordshire
c.1820
Height
7½ins:19.1cm
No mark**
A figure of Billy Waters wearing blue trousers and jacket. Price given for this example with restored violin and peg leg. Good example, £180 — £220.
£160 — £180

**Staffordshire c.1815
Height 10½ins:26.8cm. No mark**
A good equestrian group of the Duke of Wellington, holding out a baton. The modelling shows its lineage from 18th century groups quite clearly.
£400 — £500

**Walton probably 1820
Height 6ins:15.2cm. Impressed name**
A rare, royal coat of arms. The arms are those of George IV, and it was probably made to commemorate his accession in 1820. It is well potted and brightly coloured.

£300 — £400

**Staffordshire c.1820
Height 8¾ins:22.2cm. No mark**
A pair of boxers, Tom Molineaux and Tom Cribb. Cribb was "Champion of England" from 1808-24, last fighting Molineaux in September 1811 when he won both the contest and the return fight. The plain circular bases are an early sign as are the pastel tones. The modelling owes a great deal to 18th and very early 19th century Pratt figures.
£300 — £500

Staffordshire c.1820
Height 9¾ins:24.7cm
Impressed E and title
A well cast and coloured bust of Napoleon Bonaparte in the uniform of the first consul, his blue jacket edged in yellow braid. Very much in the style of Enoch Wood and possibly after a model by him. A less well executed example, £100 — £150.
£150 — £200

Staffordshire c.1840
Height 7¼ins:19.1cm. No mark
A well produced and coloured porcelain figure of a popular subject, Lord Byron, the title neatly indented from type. As it is not a contemporary subject (he died in 1824) it is not of commemorative interest and fetches less than the quality deserves.
£60 — £100

Staffordshire c.1830
Height 7¾ins. and 8ins:
19.7cm and 20.3cm
No mark
A rare pair of brightly coloured porcelain figures, probably intended as William IV and Adelaide, seated on thrones supported by the lion and unicorn. The style and colouring supports this attribution rather than that given in other reference books to the figures as being of Queen Victoria and, possibly Louis Philippe.
£100 — £150

Staffordshire c.1840
Height 6½ins:16.5cm
No mark
A very poorly modelled porcelain figure of John Wesley of little interest to collectors.
£20 — £30

Staffordshire c.1840
Height 7¾ins:19.7cm. No mark
A naïve model of Queen Victoria on horseback. One might be tempted to think that the tiny horse was a Shetland pony, the argument (specious, sadly) reinforced by the plaid saddle cloth.
£50 — £70

Staffordshire c.1840
Height 6ins:15.3cm. No mark
A rare figure of Isaac Van Amburgh, the American lion tamer who visited England in 1838, 1843 and 1848. This group combines all the qualities necessary for a high price. It is rare, theatrical, well coloured, early and titled, but would be a sure-fire winner anyway with those kitten-like lions and cuddly leopard (actually a tiger in his act).
£800 — £1,000

Left:
Staffordshire c.1840
Height 10½ins:26.7cm. No mark
A porcelain figure of Nelson, blue jacket, red breeches, gilt details, fairly common. Compare with the next example.

£50 — £80

Right:
Staffordshire c.1845
Height 8ins:20.3cm. No mark
A porcelain Nelson, a variation of the previous example and a different size, given to show how a later mould altered some of the details. The price is given for this example with broken nose. Perfect, £50 — £80.

£30 — £40

143

Staffordshire c.1840
Height 8ins:20.3cm. No mark
A good, early figure, possibly made for the Coronation in 1837. As with most early figures, the colouring is of a high standard, and these are becoming increasingly hard to find.
£60 — £80

Staffordshire c.1840
Height 8¾ins:21.6cm. No mark
A well moulded figure with bright colouring neatly titled in gilt script "Appearance is everything" and probably of theatrical origin, although it has so far defied identification. Note the number of moulds used, indicated by the separate arms, legs and base. The untitled version is also rare, £60 — £90.
£80 — £120

Staffordshire c.1841
Height 7½ins:19cm. No mark
A small but well coloured porcelain figure of Prince Albert, untitled but easily identifiable.
£30 — £50

Left:

Staffordshire c.1845
Height 10¾ins:26cm. No mark
A porcelain figure of Napoleon, well coloured but untitled. The cracks in the base affect the value. In good state, £30 — £50.
£20 — £30

Right:

Staffordshire c.1845
Height 11ins:27.9cm. No mark
A well modelled figure of Sir John Franklin the explorer who discovered the North West Passage. This figure probably commemorates either his last sighting in 1845 or the discovery of his boat, skeleton and papers in 1854. As a pair with Lady Franklin (very rare), £350 — £450. Restoration to as delicate a part as the telescope, infrequently intact, would affect the price by about 10%.
£150 — £250

Staffordshire c.1845
Height 7½ins:19.1cm. No mark

Another pair of figures of the boxers Molineux and Cribb. Quite well modelled in porcelain and carefully coloured, the titles black over impressed type. They show clearly the transition from the 18th century style (p.141) to the bolder, simpler figures of the middle of the century and later. The crack in Cribb's thigh lowers the price by about 10%.

£300 — £500

Staffordshire c.1845
Height 11ins. and 7½ins:28cm and 19cm. No mark

Two versions of Jemmy Wood, a draper in Gloucester who left £781,000 when he died. The City of Gloucester started legal proceedings claiming £20,000 from a codicil to the will. The trial disclosed many scandalous details of Wood's life. Neither of the two figures shown are particularly good; the gilt title is missing from one and badly detailed on the other. Good example, although quite common, £40 — £60.

£25 — £35 each

Staffordshire c.1845
Height 12¼ins:31.1cm. No mark

An unidentified porcelain actress, not uncommon but well modelled and coloured. The small sprigs of flowers on the bodice indicate an early date. The price is given for this model with a restored hand. Perfect, £40 — £60.

£30 — £40

Staffordshire c.1845
Height 9ins:22.9cm. No mark
An amusing pottery group of Victoria guarded by a somewhat St. Bernard-like British lion. Uncommon and with a lot of charm, the clear colouring of the lion contrasting well with the sparsely coloured queen. This example has a chipped flagstaff. Perfect, £50 — £80.
£40 — £60

Staffordshire c.1846
Height 7½ins:19.1cm. No mark
A rare and attractive figure of Ibrahim Pasha, the second son of Mehemet Ali, Pasha of Egypt, who made a state visit to England in 1846 when he was met at Portsmouth by Queen Victoria and Prince Albert. There are untitled versions of this figure which are more common, £70 — £100. Apart from its rarity, it appeals to a wide range of specialist collectors, e.g., military, royal and political.
£120 — £180

Staffordshire c.1847
Height 12ins:31.1cm. No mark
A quite rare group of Guilia Grisi as Lucrezia, and Guiseppe Mario as Gennero, and based on a music cover of 1847. The tartan kilt and flower-sprigged skirt are typical of the period. Theatrical figures are amongst the highest priced of the commemorative groups.
£100 — £150

Staffordshire c.1848
Height 7¼ins:18.3cm. No mark
A figure of William Smith O'Brien (1803-64) who led the Repeal League after breaking with O'Connell, see p.34. He led an abortive insurrection in 1848 and was transported to Tasmania. Pardoned in 1856, he died in Bangor, N. Wales. A well coloured and rare porcelain figure with a clear title.
£250 — £300

Staffordshire c.1849
Height 5ins. and 8¼ins:12.7cm and 21cm. No mark
The Potash Farm Murder set. James Blomfield Rush owned Potash Farm in Norfolk, which was mortgaged to Isaac Jermy of Stamfield Hall. Jermy demanded his money by the 30th November, 1848, but two days before the deadline expired, Rush shot him. His mistress, Emily Sandford, was forced to give evidence against him. Complete with Jermy, £500 — £700.
£400 — £500

Staffordshire c.1849
Height 8¼ins:21cm. No mark
A rare figure of the murderess Mrs. Maria Manning who, with her husband, did away with her former lover, Patrick O'Connor, burying him under the kitchen floor. They were hanged in 1849. Pair with her husband Frederick George, £350 — £450.
£140 — £180

Staffordshire mid-19th century
Height 5ins:12.8cm. No mark
This pair of porcelain children on goats are supposed to represent the royal children, the Princess Royal and the Prince of Wales; similar children on horses might well qualify but these seem unlikely. That both are apparently in girls' dresses is explained by the fact that at this period the clothing of young children was very similar. Closer inspection reveals that one wears knickers.
£80 — £120

A Minton majolica game piedish.12½ins: 32cm. Impressed Minton and date code for 1865. £150 — £200.

An earthenware soup tureen, stand and ladle, c.1835. Tureen, 12ins:30.5cm wide. Titled Chinese Flora, shield, anchor and J.B. £80 — £150; plates, £3 — £4; dishes, £5 — £20. There are too many J.B.s working in Staffordshire at this date to attribute the service.

148

Left:

Staffordshire mid-19th century
Height 4¼ins:10.8cm. No mark

A small, badly modelled and crudely cast sailor, possibly intended as Prince Alfred. The lack of a positive attribution and its poor construction make this somewhat undesirable. Many such figures lurk unloved on the shelves of junk shops all over the country.

£15 — £20

Right:

Staffordshire c.1850
Height 9¼ins:23.5cm. No mark

A figure of an unidentified actor in an unidentified role and not, therefore, of much interest. This example with one leg broken and spottily fired. Good specimen, £25 — £35.

£15 — £20

Left:

Staffordshire c.1850
Height 11ins:27.9cm. No mark

A rare figure of Joseph John Gurney standing against a pillar holding a book, titled in gilt script. A well modelled figure on an unusually complex base and of appeal to many collectors as Gurney was a Quaker philanthropist and writer who played a leading part in prison reform, negro emancipation and the abolition of capital punishment.

£200 — £250

Right:

Staffordshire c.1850
Height 14½ins:36.2cm. No mark

A relatively common model of Sir Walter Scott. This is an example where the cost of restoration, particularly difficult in the case of a dog's head, would not be justified, because the original cost, plus the cost of restoration, would be more than the cost of a good model. In good condition, £50 — £80.

£10 — £15

Staffordshire c.1850
Height 9¼ins:23.5cm. No mark
One of the most common pair of figures of the highwaymen, Tom King and Dick Turpin, and as popular now as they must have been in the 19th century. The quality varies enormously from the appalling to good, generally along date lines, the earlier the better and the price reflects this. Despite the commonness and cheapness, modern copies have been seen.

£50 — £80

Staffordshire c.1850
Height 11ins:27.9cm. No mark
An uncommon group of Sir Robert Peel, titled in gilt script. The piece probably commemorates his death after being thrown from his horse in Hyde Park in 1850. An even rarer example with his arm outstretched £1,000 + .

£200 — £300

Staffordshire c.1850
Height 12ins:30.5cm. No mark

A popular and unusual theatrical group of Othello and Iago, this example being sparsely coloured. With better coloration, £200 — £300. The figures display early characteristics with well formed and gilt title and neat features. The chipped finger and base have little effect on the price.

£100 — £150

Staffordshire c.1851
Height 9½ins:24.1cm. No mark

A porcelain figure impressed and gilt titled "Bloomers", referring to the notoriety attracted by Amelia Bloomer, who wore the pyjama-like trousers to which her name became attached. Although she never visited this country, much interest was aroused here and the fuss, rather than herself, is commemorated here.

£150 — £200

Staffordshire c.1850
Height 8¾ins:22.2cm. No mark

A popular and fairly common scene of the Death of Nelson. As with many groups that were made over a long period, the quality of the casting and colouration varies, this example moderately good; poor, £20 — £35; good, £70 — £100. It also appears in other sizes with no great effect on the price.

£50 — £70

Staffordshire c.1850
Height 15ins:38cm
No mark

A curious figure in that it was originally modelled as Benjamin Franklin but more often appears titled "Washington".

£100 — £150

151

Thomas Parr c.1851
Height 9ins. and 8½ins:22.8cm and 21.6cm
No mark

Popery and Protestantism, a pair of porcelain figures made to commemorate the "No Popery" agitation when the Pope granted territorial titles to Roman Catholic bishops. Quite rare figures and more often found singly, presumably because if you supported one side you did not purchase the other. With the present troubles in Northern Ireland these figures can still be seen to have some significance.

£150 — £200

Right:

Staffordshire c.1854
Height 11ins:27.9cm. No mark

An untitled figure of Admiral Sir Charles Napier commemorated for his part in commanding the Baltic Fleet against the Russians in the Crimean conflict. He was later relieved of his commission, his place being taken by R.S. Dundas, see p.157, and entered politics. This piece crudely cast and with broken flag at left. Better example, £70 — £100; titled, £80 — £120.

£50 — £60 as shown

Far right:

Staffordshire c.1854
Height 10¾ins:27.3cm. No mark

A porcelain figure of Michael Latas, the Turkish general who became Omar Pasha on his conversion to Islam. He is commemorated for his part in the Crimean War.

£200 — £250

Staffordshire c.1851
Height 10¾ins:27.7cm
No mark

An uncommon figure of the Hungarian, Louis Kossuth, who visited England in 1851 after a busy life promoting the Hungarian cause. This example well cast and coloured with good gilt script title.

£60 — £80

Left:
Staffordshire c.1854
Height 13¼ins:34.3cm. No mark

A relatively common military group of Napoleon III and Prince Albert, sparsely coloured and gilded. Better decorated, £40 — £60; larger example, £70 — £90.

£30 — £40

Right:
Staffordshire c.1854
Height 13¾ins:34.9cm
No mark

A good, clean figure, well coloured and with gilt title. General Sir William Codrington commanded the Light Division at Alma and Inkerman, and after 1855 was Commander in Chief of British troops in the Crimea.

£350 — £400

Staffordshire c.1854
Heights 8¼ins. and 9ins:21cm and 22.5cm. No mark

Two models of Malakoff and Sebastopol connected with the battles of the same name in the Crimean war. Not by any means well modelled or coloured, but lending some variety to a collector of military subjects. Better examples up to £60 each.

£30 — £40 each

Staffordshire c.1854
Height 13¾ins:33.6cm
No mark

A fairly complex figure of General Sir George Brown (1790-1865) who commanded the Light Division in the Crimea. This example well coloured and with raised gilt title (the "N" of Brown reversed in the mould) giving a clue to the manufacture of this particular type of raised lettering. Having modelled the original without title but with only the scroll, a mould was taken and the lettering incised into this master mould in mirror writing. Ns being particularly difficult to do backwards, the potter, who was probably only semi-literate anyway, managed all but the last. Other moulds would have been made from the master and the figures cast.

£50 — £80

Staffordshire c.1854
16¼ins:41.2cm. No mark

A large and poorly modelled but quite well coloured figure of Louis Napoleon III in blue jacket and black boots. Larger figures tend to be less expensive.

£40 — £50

Staffordshire c.1854
Height 15¾ins:40cm. No mark

A handsome military figure of Field Marshal Lord Raglan, of Crimea fame. Well cast and sparsely, but neatly, decorated. The price given is for this example, which lacks the top of one of the flags; restored, £70 — £80; perfect, £80 — £150.

£50 — £70

Staffordshire c.1854
Height 10ins:25.4cm. No mark

Two comparative examples of the same rare and desirable figure, the one on the left with clear horse's trappings and the face clear, the title less well lettered. There is little difference in date. Note the very similar sprig on the saddle cloth. Really well coloured example, £70 — £100.

£50 — £80, £40 — £60

Staffordshire c.1854
Height 10½ins:26.7cm. No mark

A reasonable example of the popular group of the three allies, Queen Victoria, Abd-ul-Medjid, Sultan of Turkey, and Napoleon III of France. Better coloured example, £80 — £120.

£60 — £80

Staffordshire c.1854
Height 10½ins:26.8cm. No mark

General Pelissier, brightly coloured and on horseback, a good combination but as the figure is not particularly rare, not a particularly high price. The impressed title is unreadable. Well titled, £80 — £120.

£60 — £80

Staffordshire c.1854
Height 9ins:22.8cm. No mark

Another General Pelissier of smaller size and of obviously cruder moulding and colouration, the title atrociously applied. Nevertheless it does have a certain vigour. With better colouring and title, £70 — £100.

£50 — £80

Staffordshire c.1855
Height 13¾ins:34.9cm. No mark

An attractively mis-titled Queen Victoria and the King of Sardinia. The use of a worn mould or boredom on the part of the decorator has led to the spelling error and as children and illiterate workers were used throughout the potteries, it is hardly surprising that mistakes occur. Better coloured, moulded and spelt, £60 — £90.

£40 — £60

Staffordshire c.1855
Height 9¼ins:23.5cm. No mark

A rare model of a very unlikely-looking Balmoral with gilt details. Purchased by Queen Victoria in 1852, it was "improved" under Prince Albert's direction and became their favourite retreat. It was the Royal Family's love of Scotland that did much to popularise things Caledonian during the second half of the century.

£80 — £100

Staffordshire c.1855
Height 12½ins:31.7cm. No mark

A very fine and rare figure of Admiral Sir Richard Saunders Dundas, well coloured and cast. The base is unusual and the details particularly well picked out. When examples such as these come on the market, the prices can be very unpredictable.

£300 — £500

Staffordshire c.1855
Height 7ins:17.8cm. No mark

A poorly produced figure of Marshal St. Arnaud who was at Alma with Lord Raglan, the title in black over a faint panel. Better and larger examples of the same figure exist, £50 — £80.

£30 — £40

Staffordshire c.1855
Height 16½ins:41.9cm. No mark

A portrait figure of R.G. Gordon-Cumming, Eton and the Cavalry, who forsook all to hunt big game in South Africa. He exhibited his trophies at the Great Exhibition and then travelled in Britain lecturing and exhibiting the skins. Environmental considerations and more reliable weapons have made lion killing a less awe-inspiring occupation than it was, but this is still an attractive and popular group, made the more appealing by Gordon-Cumming's apparent success with his claymore over a somewhat small lion cub.

£50 — £70

Staffordshire c.1856
Height 8ins:20.3cm. No mark

A group of Napoleon III, the Empress Eugenie and the Prince Imperial, their clothes well coloured. A fairly uncommon group but untitled.

£70 — £90

Staffordshire c.1860
Height 10¼ins. and 10ins:26cm and 25.4cm. No mark
The royal brothers Albert Edward and Alfred, the one in army uniform, the other naval. Titled in gilt raised capitals. Figures of this date, particularly those having large areas of enamelling, are prone to flaking detracting from the value. Since the enamel was unevenly and streakily applied, the restorer's hand can transform a scruffy example into a fine one with ease. Since there is no actual damage, head, arms, hats, etc., this form of beauty treatment is easy to miss.

£150 — £180

Staffordshire c.1860
Height 11ins:27.9cm
An attractive and uncommon group of John Brown, the anti-slaver who was hanged in 1858, with two negro children. The apparent crack on the left is in the firing and will not affect the value. Had it been damaged, £50 — £80.

£70 — £100

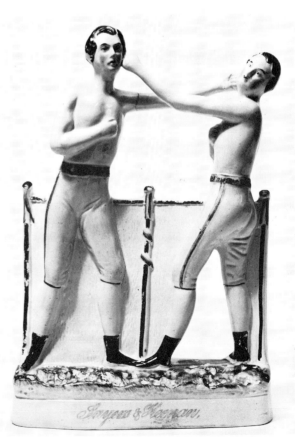

Staffordshire c.1860
Height 13ins:33cm. No mark
An extremely rare group of the boxers, John Carmel Heenan and Tom Sayers, of which only a handful of examples are known. Smaller examples of a slightly later date are more readily available, £80 — £150, as are quantities of modern reproductions which are good enough to fool the unwary (see section on "Fakes"). Compare with the earlier figures of Molineaux and Cribb (pp.141 and 145).

£250 — £300

Staffordshire c.1860
Height 12ins:30.5cm
No mark
A good example of a crisply moulded and uncoloured group of the Volunteer Rifles picked out in gilding only, except for facial details.

£35 — £45

Staffordshire c.1860
Height 11½ins:29.2cm
No mark
An uncommon and desirable theatrical subject, Jenny Lind as Alice in Meyerbeer's opera, "Robert and the Devil". Unusual for the full title in well written gilt script. More usually the subjects can be traced only through engravings in magazines or from music covers. The cross on the top of the pillar is particularly vulnerable to damage and has vanished in this example. In good condition, £120 — £180.

£70 — £90

Staffordshire
c.1860
Height 19¼ins:
48.9cm
No mark
One of the largest and most handsome Staffordshire figures, particularly when well coloured, as here. It is not, however, a commemorative figure, hence the low price.

£50 — £70

Staffordshire c.1861
Height 14¾ins:37.4cm. No mark
Another of the larger commemorative figures and one of the best. The red-shirted figure of Garibaldi beside a spirited horse, the title printed in black. Smaller versions, £60 — £80; later examples this size, invariably of poor quality, £70 — £100.

£180 — £220

Staffordshire c.1864
Height 15ins:38.1cm. No mark
An imposing and well coloured figure of Garibaldi in a somewhat unlikely pose. Common and therefore not expensive; it is paired with a figure of Shakespeare (£40 — £60) because in 1864 he visited England and Shakespeare celebrated his tricentenary.

£30 — £40

Staffordshire c.1865
Height 5¼ins:13.5cm. No mark
A schoolboy from Colston's Hospital School, founded in 1710 by Edward Colston, philanthropist. The school moved to the outskirts of Bristol in 1861 and the figure probably commemorates that event.

£60 — £80

Staffordshire
c.1865
Height 11ins:28cm
No mark
A figure of St. Francis de Sales, the patron saint of writers. While obviously not a contemporary portrait, it is very rare and desirable for collectors of religious subjects. This example is particularly well coloured.

£200 — £400

Staffordshire c.1865
Height 14ins. and 10¼ins:35.5cm and 26.1cm. No mark
Two versions of a popular and quite rare figure of a batsman, generally taken to be Julius Caesar, who played for Surrey and for England from about 1849-67. Both quite well potted and coloured but should come with a companion bowler, £250 — £350. Modern fakes do exist.

£120 — £180

Staffordshire c.1865
Height 15¼ins:38.7cm. No mark

A highly unlikely model of Abraham Lincoln on horseback adapted from another equestrian group to suit demand. The title in raised gilt capitals. This example with left foreleg cracked; a good example, better coloured, £50 — £80.

£40 — £60

Staffordshire c.1866
Height 13½ins:34.5cm

A relatively common pottery group which can be found with brighter decoration, making it more expensive, £100 — £150. At first sight a group of two sportsmen, it depicts, in fact, the murder by shooting of Thomas Smith by William Collier, when he was caught poaching. Collier was later hanged.

£40 — £60

Staffordshire c.1870
Height 12ins:31.5cm
No mark

A pair of late and badly moulded military equestrians, they are also common and sparsely coloured. They thus combine all the criteria for a low price, apart for their being undamaged. Watch out for a fake name added to the base.

£40 — £60

Staffordshire c.1870
Height 14ins:35.8cm. No mark

A poorly produced pair of figures of the second Duke of Cambridge and his actress wife, Louisa Fairbrother. The Duke was wounded in the Crimea and was nursed back to health by his wife, an act which made her popular with the masses and slightly thawed Victoria's cold shouldering of the degrading marriage. The barely visible moulded titles are sparsely gilt, the Duke is correct, but Louisa has been promoted to Duchess, to which she was not entitled.

£60 — £90

Staffordshire c.1870
Height 9½ins:24.2cm
No mark

An unusual figure of Garibaldi, the majority being mounted and of an earlier date.

£70 — £100

Staffordshire c.1871
Height 9½ins:24.2cm. No mark

A rare pair of the racing greyhounds, M'Grath and Pretender, one black and the other white, the foliage tinted and the raised capitals gilt. Master M'Grath, owned by Lord Lurgan, won the Waterloo Cup and beat Pretender in 1871.

£150 — £200

163

Staffordshire c.1871
Height 11ins:27.9cm. No mark
A wedding group of the fourth daughter of Queen Victoria, Louise Caroline Alberta, with her husband the Marquess of Lorne, later the Duke of Argyll. She would, in all probability, have received one of these groups as a gift and it would be interesting to have some record of her reaction to it as she was no mean sculptress herself.

£30 — £50

Staffordshire c.1875
Height 4¾ins:12cm. No mark
A small and poorly produced equestrian Omar Pasha, probably commemorating his death in 1871, for further information see p.152. A good example, £80 — £120.

£50 — £60

Staffordshire 1870s
Height 17¼ins. and 17¾ins:43.8cm and 45.1cm
No mark
A matched pair of pottery figures of The Queen of England and the Prince of Wales, the latter unmarked indicating a marriage. Poorly modelled in a crazed soft pottery, but the colouring better applied than one might expect at this date.

£30 — £40 each; pair, £70 — £100

Staffordshire c.1875
Height 9ins:22.8cm
No mark

A good and rare theatrical figure of Edward Askew Southern as Lord Dundreary in *Our American Cousin.* He made a great success in the part before coming to England. For a late figure the details are surprisingly complex.

£250 — £350

Staffordshire c.1880
Height 11¾ins:29.8cm. No mark

An uncommon but late figure of Prince Frederick Charles, Prince of Prussia (1828-85), who commanded the 2nd army in the Franco-Prussian War. Coloured in orange, blue and gilding, note the well detailed face.

£50 — £80

Staffordshire c.1880
Height 13¼ins:33.7cm. No mark

An unlovely pair of figures of Robert Burns and Highland Mary, the raised capital titles with almost vanished gilding. Late casts and badly coloured; better examples, £25 — £35.

£18 — £22

Staffordshire c.1885
Height 14½ins. and 14ins:
36.8cm and 36cm
No mark
A pair of equestrian figures of Lieutenant Colonel F.G. Burnaby and Major General Sir H. Stewart, killed and mortally wounded respectively in the Sudan campaign. Naïvely modelled and with little colouration these are not particularly attractive models.
£40 — £60

Staffordshire c.1900
Height 16¾ins:42.5cm
No mark
A figure of Baden-Powell, here celebrating his involvement in the Boer War and the defence of Mafeking and not the Boy Scout Movement. The pale tinted enamels and bright mercury gilding are typical as are the poor modelling, note the hands.
£30 — £45

Staffordshire c.1902
Height 12ins:30.5cm. No mark
The tail end of the Staffordshire portrait tradition, the soft pottery figures with minimal gilt decoration. Several different models exist, all fetching about the same price.
£15 — £20

Staffordshire Figures — Miscellaneous

Probably Yorkshire c.1800
Height 6¾ins:17.1cm. No mark

A rare yellow-glazed, press-moulded figure of summer. Yellow is the most desirable colour for late 18th and early 19th century wares, be they jugs, vases or figures.

£100 — £150

Staffordshire early 19th century
Height 10ins:25.4cm. No mark

A group entitled Cock Fighters actually adapted from moulds used on more common figures, the girl would normally be holding a baby or lamb. It is, nevertheless, rare and desirable, particularly as there are collectors specialising in cock fighting material.

£100 — £150

John Hall early 19th century
Height 6ins:15.4cm. No mark

A small polychrome figure of a female gardener by a spring. An unexciting object poorly produced, but gardeners are a popular subject. Pair, £80 — £120.

£30 — £50

Staffordshire
early 19th century
Height 6½ins:16.5cm. No mark

A figure of Robinson Crusoe, which although uncommon is not all that expensive as it is not strictly speaking a portrait figure.

£100 — £150

Staffordshire early 19th century
Height 5¾ins:14.7cm. No mark
A flat-backed group of a boy with his dog birds'-nesting, well cast and coloured in bright enamels.

£100 — £150

Staffordshire
early 19th century
Height 3¾ins. and 4ins:
9.5cm and 10.2cm
No mark
A pair of groups of ''Strife'' and ''Harmony'' epitomised by children fighting and kissing. Each modelled with flat back to fit on a mantelpiece.

£150 — £180

Staffordshire
early 19th century
Height 10ins:25.4cm. No mark
A pair of groups of a hairdresser and a cobbler in an *al fresco* setting, both brightly coloured and very rare.

£600 — £700

Staffordshire figure of Lady Stanhope and Dr. Meryon, 1855. 7¼ins:18.5cm. £180 — £250.

**Staffordshire
early 19th century
Height 6¼ins:15.8cm
No mark**

A rare figure of a boy sweep, riding a donkey and announcing his presence. His face totally black, the rest well coloured. Unlikely to be found in good condition; similar with small restoration, £200 — £250.

£250 — £350

**Staffordshire early 19th century
Height 7ins:17.8cm. No mark**

A rare and amusing group of a sportsman taking a very unsportsmanlike shot at close range at a perched bird, with another on the ground about to fly into the line of fire.

£250 — £300

**Wood and Caldwell early 19th century
Height 9¼ins:23.5cm
Impressed name, incised Burslem**

An attractive model of Britannia seated beside a docile lion in well painted dress, her cuirass, helmet and shield silver lustred — an unusual point. Lacks detachable metal trident. The shredded clay "moss" on the base is typical of models from the first half of the century.

£150 — £200

**Staffordshire early 19th century
Height 9¼ins:23.5cm. No mark**

A well coloured and cast example of a common subject, the Sailor's Farewell; with its companion, the Sailor's Return, it seems to have been made from about 1800 to the end of the century. The quality can vary from the appalling to the excellent as here. Pair, £150 — £180; titled pair, £180 — £220. Others from as low as £30 a pair for late, bad examples.

£40 — £70

Staffordshire early 19th century
Height 10ins:25.4cm. No mark
A rare group of a piper seated on a rock and training two dogs, dressed in hats and coats, to dance. His wife holds a third dog, the whole brightly coloured.
£300 — £400

Staffordshire first quarter 19th century
Height 10½ins:26.8cm. No mark
A group of "Old Age" modelled in typical low-fired, soft biscuit-like clay and brightly coloured. A not uncommon group and unattractive to boot.
£150 — £180

Staffordshire first quarter 19th century
Height 8¾ins:22.3cm. No mark
A spill vase group of two men sheltering under a hollow tree, the branches of which form vases. In the crook of each branch is either a bird in a nest or an inappropriate model of a mourning girl.
£150 — £200

171

Probably Walton c.1820
Height 6½ins:16.5cm. No mark
A pair of brightly coloured groups of gardeners under a tree. The majority of Walton's groups are marked with an impressed name on a scroll at the rear of the group.

£120 — £180

Possibly Don c.1820
Height 10¼ins:26cm
No mark
An attractive pottery church crisply cast and coloured, the painter adding the unlikely detail of two winding holes for a key in the clock face. Restoration to the finials and tower top would be acceptable and not affect the price dramatically.

£100 — £150

Dixon, Austin and Co., Sunderland 1820-1826
Height 9ins:22.9cm. Impressed name

A rare set of the seasons with coloured details and areas of silver lustre, the titles in black. Sets of figures are obviously much rarer than odd singles which sell for £120 — £150.

£1,000 — £1,500

Staffordshire c.1825
Height 6½ins:16.5cm
No mark

A pair of children reading, crudely modelled and simply coloured.

£80 — £100

Staffordshire c.1825
Height 7¼ins:18.4cm. No mark
A group of Remus and Romulus, the two babies suckling a large wolf, on a blue scrolled green base, lacking the bocage behind. Complete example, £150 — £250.
£80 — £120

Staffordshire
c.1830
Height 10½ins:
26.7cm
No mark
A pair of silver lustre figures of Apollo and Diana, naïvely modelled in red earthenware under a worn silver lustre. Pair in better condition, £200 — £250.
£140 — £180

Staffordshire
c.1830
Height 8ins:20.3cm
No mark
A rare pottery Sergeant from the 80th Staffordshire Volunteers wearing brightly coloured uniform.
£150 — £180

**Staffordshire
c.1830
Height 7ins:17.8cm
No mark**
A figure of a Scots beggar with peg leg, playing inaccurate bag-pipes, his clothes brightly coloured.
£120 — £140

**Staffordshire c.1830-1835
Height 3½ins:8.8cm. No mark**
A crude group of the babes in the wood asleep in a grotto, the top forming three vases. Many of these groups from the first half of the 19th century are constructed by press moulding, shown by the sharp mould line running round the edge of the piece.
£60 — £80

**Staffordshire c.1835
Height 16¼ins:41.3cm. No mark**
A large and well modelled and decorated figure of the Flagellation of Christ, marking a transition from the early 19th century style to the representative portrait figure. Inexpensive because of the subject, not through any lack of quality.
£30 — £40

**Staffordshire c.1835
Height 11¼ins:28.6cm. No mark**
A figure of St. Peter holding the keys to heaven and a sword, the biblical allusions further reinforced by the cockerel by his side.
£100 — £150

Above and above right: **Obadiah Sherrat c.1840**
Height 8ins:20.3cm. No mark

An attractive and rare pair of temperance groups, the one on the left impressed "Tee Total", a term coined in 1834, depicting domestic bliss, the other "Ale Bench", showing the dreadful consequences of alcohol. Both amusingly modelled and well coloured. With so much detail these groups are invariably damaged and the price given is for the pair of groups with some restoration. Good examples, £1,000 — £1,500.

Obadiah Sherrat is recorded as working from about 1815-28 at Hot Lane, Burslem. He then moved to Waterloo Road. He died in 1840, but the business was continued by his son Hamlet until 1854. There is no reason to suppose that all the footed groups are early on in the century, the example illustrated supporting this contension, and many must have been made from the original moulds by his son. Unless the pot on the bench is a coffee pot, which is unlikely, its shape must be c.1840.

£800 — £1,000

Staffordshire
Probably second quarter 19th century
Height 8ins:20.3cm. No mark

A rather dreadful silver lustre figure of "Plenty", after a model (a long way after) by Ralph Wood. A misuse of silver lustre which only detracts from the original modelling leaving it looking like over-polished pewter. Exact dating very difficult but conceivably even later than that given.

£50 — £80

Staffordshire mid-19th century
Height 6½ins:16.5cm. No mark

A rare group of two young cricketers, simply modelled but brightly coloured. Cricketing subjects are always popular even when, as here, unidentified. pair with companion group, £400 — £500.

£160 — £200

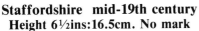

Staffordshire c.1850
Height 4½ins:11.5cm. No mark

A porcellaneous figure whose only interest lies in its almost unparalleled awfulness. It is hard to believe that it would ever be bought by a serious collector. However, for those of a less serious nature some little pleasure might be squeezed by trying to solve the enigma posed by the figure with its tantalisingly blank title panel. Was it originally modelled as a woman, Isabella mourning at her pot of basil, perhaps? Is it ennui not misery depicted? Maybe the moustache was added to satisfy the demand for an actor in a tragic part.

£10 — £15

Staffordshire c.1850
height 6¾ins:17.2cm. No mark

A small equestrian officer of naïve conception, brightly coloured and untitled. Cheap because of the anonymity. It is quite possible that a titled example will one day appear since the moulds were occasionally used for more than one "hero" but the price would depend upon who was depicted.

£10 — £15

Staffordshire c.1850
Height 5ins:12.7cm. No mark
A small and fairly common group of
an unidentified subject. The clothing
suggests a theatrical subject and a
definite attribution — the discovery of
a print of the same pose for example —
would raise the price, probably to £40
— £60 in the first instance.
£5 — £10

Staffordshire c.1860
Height 11¼ins:28.6cm. No mark
An old testament subject of Saul presenting his daughter to
David, and so titled in gilt script. The figures poorly
modelled and not well coloured. Old Testament collecting
is a neglected field, and a comprehensive collection could
be built quite cheaply. These groups do not fall within the
scope of religious portrait collectors.
£30 — £40

Staffordshire c.1860
Height 6½ins. and 6¾ins:
16.5cm and 17.2cm
No mark
A rare pair of figures entitled in
gilt script "Colin" and "Flora",
their clothes well coloured.
Taken from a print but not of
interest to a commemorative
collector.
£125 — £150

Staffordshire c.1860
Height 13ins:33cm
No mark

One of the commonest Staffordshire groups, The Rivals. More commonly found less well coloured, £8 — £12, or white and gilt only, £5 — £10. Poor examples can be found for under £5.

£10 — £15

Staffordshire c.1860
Height 13¾ins:35cm
No mark

A rare figure and an interesting subject, well modelled and coloured, although the enamel is flaking. Same in good condition, £100 — £120.

£100 — £150

Staffordshire c.1870
Height 8½ins. and 8¾ins:21.6cm and 22.2cm. No mark

A pair of jockeys remaining at present unidentified. Not very well coloured and quite common. A genuinely titled example, if such exists, could be worth £120 — £150 for a single figure. There are many late and modern copies.

£50 — £70

Staffordshire c.1870 and late 19th century
Height 6¾ins. and 7½ins:17.2cm and 19.1cm. No mark

An interesting example of a degeneration in quality. The building, as yet unidentified, is crisply moulded and boldly decorated, the glaze thick with widish crazing; the other later example is badly decorated with a discoloured fine crackle. Early, £20 — £30; late, £8 — £10.

Staffordshire late 19th century
Height 12ins:30.5cm. No mark

A crudely cast castle facade watch holder, made to take a pocket watch during the night. This example demonstrates the worst features of late pieces; poor casting, bad painting and gilding, all on a discoloured and crazed body. The same mould better executed, £15 — £20.

£4 — £6

Staffordshire late 19th century
Height 13ins:33cm. No mark

A spill holder in the form of Dog Tray and his master, the title in worn gilt capitals. Tray was a popular name for dogs throughout the century and was immortalised in song. This example with the dog's neck cracked; good example, £35 — £40.

£30 — £35

Tea and Coffee Wares

At the turn of the nineteenth century tea bowls were going out of fashion and cups were mainly used. Nevertheless, as late as 1820 services were being made in earthenware with tea bowls. The wealthiest families used porcelain cups and saucers (tea plates did not appear till the 1870s) and silver tea pot, milk jug and sucrier. Those slightly lower down the social scale might aspire to a porcelain tea pot or jug, but the majority of the population used earthenware services. Being much softer, the major pieces in earthenware have rarely survived and are much sought after. There is a growing interest in this first half of the century and collectors are searching out marked specimens or patterns from known factories.

Where the jug or mug was the usual item to bear messages or thanks, the potter seems to have reserved the tea pot for his wildest flights of fancy, and not only in the nineteenth century. The tradition goes back several centuries to China and some extremely bizarre pots were made in the eighteenth century by most of the major English and Continental factories. In the first half of the nineteenth century the potters seem to have been fairly restrained. The most unusual pots were perhaps those pretending to be silver but failing badly as the soft pottery was unsuitable for producing the sharp edges of the styles of the time, and they invariably got the proportions wrong. Anyway silver lustre (actually platinum) does not look like silver. Fancy ran riot with the oriental-based designs that came in with majolica in the 1860s and some wonderful pieces were made and which are now racing up in price. There are also collectors solely of tea pots.

The tradition did not die with the twentieth century; some weird examples appeared in the 1920s and 30s (for example the racing car pot on p.187) and even the tea bag has failed to kill it off. Carlton Ware are issuing a whole series of domestic wares, albeit in porcelain, which stand on feet and which must surely be avidly collected in the future.

Staffordshire c.1810
Diameter 4ins:10.2cm. No mark
An unusual saucer in silver lustre on a yellow ground.
With its matching coffee can, £80 — £100.
£20 — £30

Castleford type 1810-1815
Height 12¾ins:38cm. No mark

A smear-glazed porcellaneous stoneware coffee pot moulded with "Plenty" on one side and an American eagle on the other, the lines in blue enamel. Uncommon, particularly in good condition but without a devoted following, although this is growing. Similar pot but without the eagle, £160 — £180.

£240 — £280

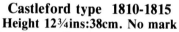

Staffordshire c.1815
Diameter 2¾ins:7cm. No mark

A tea bowl printed in puce with a child learning to write, the rim red. With saucer, £25 — £35.

£8 — £12

Shorthose & Co. 1817-1822
Diameter of saucer 4½ins:11.5cm
Printed SHORTHOSE

An uncommon black-printed tea bowl and saucer. The rustic scene and flower border hand coloured in red, yellow, green and blue, orange rim. Earthenware tea bowls of this period are much sought after, particularly when marked. Uncoloured example, £10 — £15.

£15 — £20

Staffordshire c.1825
Height 11ins:27.9cm. No mark

A black basalt tea pot, the knop a direct copy of a Wedgwood "widow" original. Not uncommon and not much in demand. Marked Wedgwood example, £60 — £80.

£18 — £22

Spode c.1830
Height 8ins:20.3cm. Impressed name

A treacle-brown glazed Cadogan tea pot, named after wine pots bought back from China by the Hon. Mrs. Cadogan at the end of the 18th century, and presumably first used by her. The tea was made in another receptacle and the pot was filled through a hole in the base, entering the body through an internal tube. On inverting the pot the tea was therefore contained and could come out only through the spout. It must have been a great novelty at the time, proving a boon when conversation flagged at tea parties.

£25 — £ 35

J. and R. Clews c.1825
Plate diameter 6¾ins:17cm. Bowl height 5¼ins:13.2cm. Impressed crown and circle

A plate and two bowls made for export to the United States and transfer printed in blue with ships, including a paddle steamer, approaching a harbour and titled "The landing of General Lafayette at Castle Garden, New York, 1824". These pieces would have been produced almost immediately on hearing the news and shipped back for sale as soon as possible.

Plate £100 — £150; bowls £40 — £60

J. and R. Clews c.1830
Tea pot height 7½ins:19cm. Sucrier height 6½ins:16.5cm. Impressed crown and circle
A blue printed tea pot and sucrier with the American eagle against clouds and flowers. Clews produced a considerable amount of blue printed earthenware for the American market, see pp.122 and 183.
£120 — £150 and £80 — £120

Enoch Wood & Sons c.1830
Height 12ins:30.5cm. No mark
A coffee pot printed in blue with scenes of a man fishing on the banks of a river, a country residence in the background, which to save the cost of re-engraving the plate, has been used upside down on the cover and shoulders. A definite attribution to an American view would more than double the price.

£70 — £100

Staffordshire 1840-1850
Height 9ins:22.9cm. No mark
A tea kettle, the dark red clay covered in a copper lustre and almost certainly based on a copper original. Tea kettles had the tea made in them and were not used for boiling water.

£80 — £120

Sunderland mid-19th century
Diameter 7ins:17.8cm. No mark
A Sunderland lustre pottery bowl painted with brightly coloured and pink lustred flowers. A very basic bowl with not much to recommend it, hence the low price.
£5 — £8

Minton 1867-1868
Impressed name and date code
A highly distinctive majolica tête-a-tête in Chinese taste, well moulded in the form of fruits and flowers and glazed in straw, green, brown and pink. A number of factories apart from Minton produced more or less bizarre table wares, many of which can never have been used. They rank amongst the most interesting and important designs of the period. 1867-68 is early for such a display of the naturalistic appreciation that was to lead on to art nouveau. It is probable that as the period becomes better understood, pieces such as this that break new ground historically will rise in value faster than most, particularly, as in this case, when also attractive.
£300 — £350

Royal Worcester 1874
Height 8¼ins:21cm
Impressed and printed circle marks
and date
A good tea pot neatly joining the Chinese and Japanese cultures. The former has lent the shape from a redware or *yi hsing* example and the latter the brilliantly enamelled and gilt diaper and *cash* over black transfer outlines. The handle turquoise. Not of much interest to Royal Worcester collectors but an early examples of "Japonaise" for devotees of the style.
£100 — £120

Mintons 1874
Height 7¼ins:19.1.cm. Impressed name and date

A good example of Minton humour, the Chinaman's head removable to form a cover. The clay used for these pots and many majolica wares of this period is very soft and few seem to have survived intact. A really crisply moulded example, well coloured and undamaged could fetch £150 — £200. Similar idea of monkey grasping a nut, £200 — £250.

£120 — £150

"Derbyshire" c.1885
8½ins. to 11¾ins:21.6cm to 29.8cm. No mark

So called "Derbyshire", so called "barge" tea pots. These large pots were made mainly for the bargees plying the canals, who were attracted by the bright moulded flowers shown off by the treacle-brown ground. They are frequently found with messages impressed from type, occasionally made-to-measure as on the outside examples, "A present from Burton, 1884" and "From Mr & Mrs Jackson to Mr & Mrs Terry". Now very much in demand by the return to nature movement and often found photographed in the glossies along with stripped pine, rush matting and stone-ground bread.

£50 — £80 for ordinary types as on the right and left.
More unusual £80 — £100

Derbyshire 1888
Height 7¼ins:18.4cm. No mark
A rare barge tea pot with twin spouts for pouring two cups at the same time and bearing a message impressed from type, the reverse reads "By her loving son Henry Thomason 1888".

£70 — £90

Doulton Burslem c.1890
Height 8½ins:21.5cm. Printed mark, see text
An earthenware tea pot with original silver plated cover, the body printed in brown and hand coloured with flowers. The mark reads "Royle's Patent Self-pouring, No. 6237, 1886, Manufactured by Doulton Burslem for JJ Royle, Manchester." The pot works by placing a cup under the spout and raising the lid, which has a long cylindrical sleeve attached. Then, with the index finger over the hole in the knop, the lid is depressed which forces the tea out by air pressure. Queen Victoria is known to have used one of the pots and it caused some excitement at the Chicago Exhibition of 1893.

£20 — £30

James Sadler & Sons
1930s
Height 8¼ins:20.9cm
Impressed
MADE IN ENGLAND
An amusing earthenware teapot in the form of a racing car under bright-green glaze with silver lustre details. Can be found in other colours and forms such as an aeroplane. Becoming more desirable from the interest in automobilia, art deco and kitsch.

£30 — £40

*A pearlware tea pot with the Cordwainers' (shoemakers) Arms on one side and a
dedication on the other, 1803. 5ins:12.8cm. £120 — £140.*

A Staffordshire tea pot, c.1880. 11ins:28cm. £40 — £60.

Vases

A comparison with *The Price Guide to 19th and 20th Century British Porcelain* will reveal a striking difference in the number of vases illustrated in the two books. The number in the *Price Guide to Porcelain* reflects the emphasis that was placed on the vase as a non-utilitarian object on which a great deal of effort could be expended. Porcelain was a more appropriate material on which to lavish this attention, hence the far larger number illustrated in the previous book. There is also difference in the date distribution, most pottery vases of interest coming from the first half of the century, most in porcelain from the second half.

At the beginning of the nineteenth century Masons were producing many fine stoneware vases, mostly after Chinese originals, and since there is a very healthy interest in Mason's products, several of these have been included. Apart from some transfer printed and hand coloured vases, possibly produced by Pratt, some classical designs in black on coloured grounds which could be by Samuel Alcock, and wares by Charles Meigh, who made a few superbly painted stoneware vases for the Great Exhibition, the vase as an art form seems to have been neglected. The renaissance came, as in so many other fields, with majolica, although even here other forms often took the designer's eye.

At the end of the century a few minor factories attempted copying the finer painted wares of Royal Worcester on earthenware with a conspicuous lack of success.

G.M. and C.J. Mason 1813-1829
Height 16ins:40.6cm. Printed name
A large chinoiserie vase, fluted and transfer printed in black, well touched with enamels and based on a late 18th century Chinese original. Pair, £250 — £300.
£100 — £120

Possibly Leeds c.1815-1820
Height 6¼ins:15.9cm. No mark

A vase of campana form, decorated with coloured stylised flowers and leaves, reserved on a pink lustre ground. The white areas were drawn in wax before the lustre was applied, and the tendrils scratched on afterwards. Stencils were also used. Pair, £350 — £380.

£100 — £120

Possibly Leeds c.1825
Height 6¼ins:15.9cm. No mark

A vase decorated in silver resist with stylised flowers, the base moulded with wheat ears. Pair, £120 — £150.

£40 — £50

Possibly G.M. and C.J. Mason c.1825
Height 4½ins:11.4cm. No mark

A miniature vase painted with chinamen on a mirror black ground. An uncommon object of appeal to both Mason collectors and those of miniature objects.

£35 — £45

G.M. and C.J. Mason c.1825
Height 9½ins:24cm. Impressed Patent Ironstone China

An ironstone urn painted in *famille rose* enamels with pseudo Chinese flowers, the blue ground with gilt scrolls. Pair, £120 — £150.

£40 — £60

Probably
G.M. and C.J. Mason
c.1825
Height 17¼ins:43.8cm
No mark

An amusing vase and cover painted with bold flowers on the somewhat bizarre body. The awkward conception of many of the vases of this period makes them difficult to love, and they are even spurned by the decorators. Only a setting such as the Brighton Pavilion can really do them justice. Pair, £220 — £350.

£60 — £80

G.M. and C.J. Mason c.1825
Height 26½ins:67.3cm. No mark

Although not marked, these are easily recognisable as Masons ironstone and typical of the bizarre, if not ugly, design of the pre-Victorian era. The design is based on ill-understood Chinese and the pattern is Imari in iron-red, blue and gilding. The handles, which would have originally been dragons, have changed into dolphins. The shape of the pagoda-form cover can be found on Jacob-Petit scent bottles of the same date. Pair, £300 — £400.

£100 — £150

Staffordshire c.1830
Height 18¾ins:47.5cm. Pseudo Oriental seal

An interesting pair of earthenware vases transfer printed with Chinese warriors, pseudo calligraphy and flowers. Probably not Masons, and being unmarked and in earthenware, not stoneware, they will not fetch a Masons price. The engraving of the original plate has gone to extraordinary pains to copy the Chinese characters, some of which are close enough to the original to be readable.

£220 — £250

Left:

Staffordshire c.1830
Height 5¾ins:14.5cm. No mark

A good quality black ground vase painted with bright flowers and leaves, the whole having the appearance of enamelled black basalts which it is probably trying to imitate (see the Wedgwood examples on p.220). The result is not unsuccessful. Pair, £60 — £80.

£25 — £35

Right:

Possibly F. and R. Pratt & Co. c.1835
Height 23ins:58.4cm. No mark

An earthenware vase and lid, lacking its over cover, its original function being for pot-pourri. The flowers in bright enamels, hand painted over a transfer print. Pair complete with covers and lids, £120 — £150. Since the colouration is not wholly printed even a solid attribution to the Pratt factory would not make them of interest to pot-lid collectors with the usual attendant rise in price.

£30 — £50

Left:

William Ridgway and Co. c.1835
Height 25½ins:64.8cm
Impressed shield and initials

A large very decorative "opaque granite china" (actually a form of stoneware) vase and cover, hand coloured over a transfer printed outline with chinoiserie flowers and butterflies. Very much an interior decorator's piece. Pair, £250 — £350.

£100 — £120

Right:

Possibly F. and R. Pratt & Co. c.1845
Height 14½ins:36.8cm. No mark

A brown-ground vase, transfer printed in colours, the handles gilt. This example with cracked foot; in good state, £8 — £10; pair, £20 — £25. These pseudo-classical vases and urns often have bright blue, red or brown grounds, with a white design overprinted in black, and with other enamels added by hand. They fall into no collecting bracket, nor are they very decorative.

£3 — £5

A large Mason's ironstone vase printed in brown and hand coloured,
c.1825. 21ins:53cm. £120 — £150. Pair £300 — £500.

**Probably Welsh
Mid-19th century
Height 6¾ins:17.2cm
No mark**

A vase printed on one side with a clock face and on the other with Hope, the ground copper lustre. The families in which a vase such as this was likely to be displayed, would not have been able to afford a clock, time was apportioned by the church clock and rousing undertaken by a professional roundsman banging on doors or windows, or even, if Thomas Hardy is to be believed, by the pulling of strings attached to toes. This pseudo clock was perhaps meant to impress passers by or as a self-directed joke.

£30 — £50

**Staffordshire c.1850
Height 25¼ins:64.1cm. No mark**

A large pot-pourri vase, cover and lid, printed and hand coloured with fruit on a raspberry-red ground. An unattractive shape with undertones of the fairground prize although the quality of production is of a quite high standard. Large, anonymous vases of this type are not popular. Pair, £120 — £150.

£40 — £60

**Charles James Mason 1851
Height 13¾ins:34.9cm
Printed pelmet and 1851 Exhibition**

A pair of ironstone vases based on Chinese originals and printed in black and hand coloured with Buddhist lions and clouds, the handles gilt. The 1851 Exhibition mark found on the base of these vases is rarely met with, but these are not from the much admired G.M. & C.J. Mason of Patent Ironstone fame, but a much later (1851-54) Daisy Bank, Longton works. The quality is not as high and the style is that of thirty years earlier. It is little wonder that Charles Mason was having financial difficulties when he was trying to sell long superseded designs.

£250 — £350

Minton c.1855
Height 22½ins:57cm. No mark

A well modelled vase and cover painted with brightly coloured Bacchic putti, probably based on an 18th century Italian porcelain original.

£200 — £300

Hill Pottery Company c.1855
Height 16¼ins:41.3cm. Printed monogram

A pair of vases with terracotta-coloured ground printed with design based on the Portland vase. Well produced but, like the example on p.192 (bottom right), not much appreciated. This pair have the advantage of being of good quality and of a large size making them ideal for decoration. Their time will come.

£80 — £120

Possibly F. & R. Pratt c.1870
Height 17½ins:44.5cm. No mark

The finely crackled, pink ground vases are printed in grey and hand coloured, the mouth and foot with gilt lines. Numbers of these anonymous vases, usually not of this size or quality, appear on the market, and some can be attributed to Pratt. Less decorative examples from £30 a pair.

£80 — £120

195

Royal Worcester 1871
Height 11¾ins:29.8cm
Printed and impressed mark and date code
An unusual pair of vases painted in *famille rose* enamels, with cranes between moulded gilt feet and mask handles. This pair has chips to the feet. Perfect pair, £180 — £220.

£160 — £200

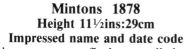

Mintons 1878
Height 11½ins:29cm
Impressed name and date code
An earthenware moon flask enamelled with wild flowers on the reddish-brown body. The neck with black and gilt key-fret. The shape was more usually made in porcelain where the quality of painting is often better. Pair, £150 — £200.

£60 — £80

Mintons 1876
Height 19ins:48.3cm. Impressed Mintons and date code
A pair of large earthenware vases painted in his typical palette of browns, cream and sombre colours by William Mussill, signed, the slips applied very thickly, almost like oil paint. The design of the vases with their elephant head and ring handles and diaper borders, is based on contemporary Japanese examples. These vases are good examples of Japanese taste in this country. Mussill's naturalistic style and drab colouration prevent them from reaching the high price bracket that they really warrant.

£500 — £600

**Pinder, Bourne and Co.
c.1880**
Impressed Pinder, Bourne and Co.
A well produced pair of moon flasks from a factory not normally associated with such pieces, the lapwings and snipe naturalistically painted. Very decorative and surprisingly inexpensive.

£140 — £180

Royal Worcester c.1880
Height 9¼ins:23cm. Impressed mark
A ridiculous vase in the form of a Japanese boy peering down at a grotesque face looking out from a tree stump. All glazed in tones of blue and brown. Like all Royal Worcester earthenware, not highly prized at the moment, this more deservedly so than most. The model is probably based on a contemporary Japanese bronze or earthenware original.

£30 — £40

Staffordshire c.1890
Height 8ins:20.3cm. No mark
The maker of this hideous object rightly preferred to remain anonymous. It must rank as the worst travesty of the Babarini or Portland Vase ever made. Crudely potted in buff clay under a streaky brown and olive glaze, the figures in low relief.

£2 — £3

Right:

Langley late 19th century
Height 9¾ins:24.8cm
Impressed name

A stoneware vase incised with a view of Stratford Church and coloured, the blue borders with gilt foliage. The whole is very closely based on Doulton stoneware of the period and is part of a three piece garniture, £80 — £120. Apart from mass-produced pieces, Langley ware is rarely met with which explains the low price.

£20 — £30

Doulton & Co. c.1892
Height 14¾ins:37.4cm. Printed Doulton Burslem
A vase painted in rust monochrome by John P. Hewitt, signed. The naturalistic technique is better suited to porcelain and up till recently these vases have fallen unhappily between the buyers of decorative wares and those of Doulton studio pieces. A growing interest from America is changing the picture and prices are rising. The subject will be more fully dealt with in *The Price Guide to Art and Studio Pottery*.

£180 — £250

Doulton & Co. c.1890
Height 22½ins:57cm. Printed name
A very large vase painted with greyhounds by Henry Mitchell, signed, the neck and foot apricot, red and gilt. The base bears the retailer's mark of Phillips of Oxford Street and dessert services are known with similar dogs by Mitchell. Plates, £30 — £40.

£300 — £400

Carltonware 1920s
Height 12½ins:31.7cm. Printed name
A large jar and cover with a printed gilt design of
Egyptian inspiration, coloured in bright enamels
on a mottled blue ground. The technique is typical
of the factory of this period and relates to the
Wedgwood fairyland designs, most of which are
on porcelain. Underpriced at the moment given its
quality.

£120 — £150

S. Fielding and Co. c.1920
Vase height 10¼ins:26cm. Printed Crown Devon
An example of a minor factory attempting, unsuccessfully, to produce an answer to Royal Worcester ware painted
by James Stinton, see the *Price Guide to 19th and 20th Century British Porcelain,* but on an earthenware body.
These, signed by G. Cox, are by no means as good.

£80 — £120

Wedgwood

The Wedgwood factory has been given a section to itself as it forms a readily identifiable unit. Any piece that is unmarked is either not accepted as Wedgwood or fetches a considerably lower price. The north American continent has venerated Wedgwood as *the* English pottery since the late eighteenth century when large quantities were shipped over for everyday use. Many of the best collections of eighteenth century Wedgwood have been formed in the United States and Americans are still buying the best pieces of the last two centuries as well as modern products. They are also absorbing large quantities of less important examples, particularly if of classic form, such as the vase bottom left on p.222. In the century that concerns us, their taste is for basalt and jasper, the Portland vase remaining in both a strong favourite, as well as for plaques, vases and the occasional dish. Three-coloured jasper is at a high premium because of its rarity. There was until a few years ago a resistance to many innovations of the factory during the nineteenth century such as majolica but these are, at last, and quite rightly, being given proper consideration and prices are rising. However, the very large pieces (over about sixteen inches) can be difficult to sell. A few of the individually painted wares of the twentieth century have been included although they more properly belong in a price guide to Studio Pottery. Fairyland and other lustres have already been dealt with in the companion *Price Guide to English Porcelain* but are represented here by one early dish on an earthenware body.

Jasper and basalt are a great deal easier to restore than glazed earthenware, so examine all potential purchases carefully, if necessary using a pin.

This section has been split into two sections, "Earthenware, Redware" up to p. 219, and "Jasper and Basalt" from p. 220. The Portland Vase appears at the end of the section on p.232.

Wedgwood: Earthenware, Redware

Josiah Wedgwood c.1800
Height 3¾ins:9.5cm. Impressed name
A rare miniature redware tea pot and cover painted in *famille rose* enamels after a Chinese original. Ideal cabinet object for a collector with limited space.

£60 — £80

Josiah Wedgwood c.1800
Height 10ins:25.4cm. Impressed name
A pearlware figure wearing black hat, brown waistcoat and
yellow breeches. The mark makes all the difference to the price.
Unmarked example, £120 — £150.
£200 — £250

Josiah Wedgwood c.1810
Height tea pot:6⅞ins:17.5cm. Impressed Wedgwood
A dreary caneware tea pot, cover and stand, the yellow-brown
body sprigged with grey vine. Uncommon but like much
caneware dirty-looking. Better example, £100 — £150.
£70 — £100

Josiah Wedgwood early 19th century
Height 6ins:15.2cm
Impressed Josiah Wedgwood, Feb 2nd, 1805
A very rare incense burner and cover on the back of three
dolphins. The body moulded in dark red clay and covered with a
copper lustre. This is a well-known pattern but the mark has not
been satisfactorily explained. It appears only on incense burners
and tripod stands. An unmarked example, £400 — £500; a
similar object (not a known Wedgwood design), £80 — £120.
£700 — £900

Josiah Wedgwood c.1815
Height 4¼ins:10.8cm
Impressed Wedgwood
A rare flower holder with detachable pierced cover covered in the so-called Moonlight, mottled pink lustre.
£350 — £380

Josiah Wedgwood c.1830
Impressed name
A cream glazed breakfast service moulded with flowering twigs. The price given for twelve each of large and small cups, each with saucers, two muffin dishes and covers, sugar bowl and cover, cream jug and bowl.
£300 — £400 (service)

Josiah Wedgwood c.1830
Height 4ins:10.2cm
Impressed name
A curiously designed milk jug in red stoneware, glazed inside and brightly enamelled with flowers on the exterior.
£20 — £30

Josiah Wedgwood c.1830
Length 12½ins:31cm. Impressed name
An earthenware bidet transfer printed in pale blue with the same eastern scene used twice. Although not common, too large an item for most collectors and outside the Wedgwood devotees' scope. As the decoration is on the inside (originally it would have fitted in a mahogany stand covering the sides) it is difficult to display to advantage.

£50 — £60

Josiah Wedgwood c.1830-1840
Height 8¼ins:20.9cm. Impressed name
A *rosso antico* tea pot, the red body with classical figures in black relief.
£100 — £150

Josiah Wedgwood c.1830
Impressed name
An earthenware plate and tureen printed in blue with a chinoiserie scene in a floral border. Quite crisp transfer printing but not an exciting subject. Typical of those of most factories of the period, here the normally magic Wedgwood name makes less difference than usual to the price. Soup tureen, £50 — £80; sauce tureen, £30 — £50; vegetable dish, £10 — £15; plates, £1 — £2; meat dishes, £3 — £30 depending on size.

Plate £10 — £15
Tureen £40 — £60

A Wedgwood rosso antiquo *tea pot, c.1815. Height 4½ins:11.4cm. Impressed Wedgwood. With chipped spout, £150 — £200; in good condition, £200 — £300.*

A Wedgwood glazed caneware infuser, the interior with two strainers, 1810-15. 7¼ins:18.4cm. Impressed Wedgwood. £120 — £140.

A Wedgwood green jasper dip plaque, c.1830. 6ins:15.2cm. £80 — £150.

Right: A Wedgwood earthenware jug and beakers printed with Punch subjects, 1927. Jug 10ins:25.5cm. Impressed Wedgwood. Beaker, £8 — £10; jug, £12 — £18.

Josiah Wedgwood c.1840
Height 5¾ins:14.6cm. Impressed name
A good *rosso antico* jug, the terracotta body
applied with black putti below fruiting vine. Jugs
of this type are not common and, like all *rosso
antico,* much sought after by collectors.
£180 — £220

Josiah Wedgwood c.1830
Height overall 15ins:38.1cm. Impressed name
A red stoneware tea pot of unusual but unappreciated form.
A large number of interesting designs were produced between
1830 and 1850 which have not survived in any great
quantities, probably one of the few possible areas left in
which to build a representative collection of Wedgwood.
£15 — £20

Josiah Wedgwood c.1840-1850
Height 9½ins:21.1cm
Impressed name
An attractively simple tea pot in
brown stoneware applied with a
glazed blue grape vine. Matching
service of six cups and saucers, milk
jug, basin, and sucrier, £120 —
£180. Compare with the caneware
example on p.202.
£20 — £30

205

Josiah Wedgwood 1840-1900
12ins:30.5cm. Impressed name

A game pie dish in a buff biscuit-like clay, moulded with dead birds on grape vine. It should come with a liner and was made for kitchen to table use. Because many have been used in the oven, they are often found discoloured with a considerable reduction in price. Compare with glazed example on p.213. Unmarked, £10 — £15.

£40 — £60

Josiah Wedgwood mid-19th century
Height 17½ins:44.5cm. Impressed name

A large bust of Minerva, goddess of war, her helmet and cuirass silvered. Although rare such large coloured earthenware busts are not popular. The same in black basalt, £600 — £800.

£200 — £250

Josiah Wedgwood mid-19th century
5¼ins:13.3cm. Impressed Wedgwood

A *rosso antico* bowl applied with black Egyptianesque reliefs. The crocodiles at the left and right were a frequent motif and also appear as knops. Pair, £150 — £180.

£60 — £80

Josiah Wedgwood
Third quarter of the 19th century
Height 12ins:30.5cm. Impressed Wedgwood

A pair of earthenware vases, the turquoise and rust bodies well applied in white and under a glassy glaze. Less common than similar pieces in jasper or basalt, but fetching about the same price.

£700 — £900

Josiah Wedgwood
Third quarter of the 19th century
Height 14¾ins:37.4cm. Impressed name

A rare vase painted with the Duchess of Devonshire and Child after Reynolds, the moulded leaves and handles bronzed and gilded. Outside the normal range of Wedgwood collectors and therefore not as expensive as it might be, but with taste changing such pieces could be in for a rapid rise in price.

£220 — £280

Josiah Wedgwood c.1860
Diameter 21ins:53.3cm. Impressed name

A very large earthenware plaque painted by Emile Lessore, signed, with the Rape of Europa.

£800 — £1,200

Josiah Wedgwood c.1860
Diameter 9¼ins:23.4cm. Impressed name

An attractive earthenware plate painted by Emile Lessore and signed. Scalloped plates in a body as soft as this are very prone to chips which, when bordered in yellow or brown as here, are easy to restore. Pair, £380 — £450.

£180 — £220

Josiah Wedgwood 1868
Diameter 9¼ins:23.4cm. Impressed name and date code

A plate of the same form as the last but without the magic of Lessore's name and painted, probably by an assistant of his as the technique is very similar, with a cartoon from *Punch*. The reverse bears the *Punch* line: "Hey, Colin! Dinna ye ken the watter's for drinking, And nae for bathing?" Cartoons appearing on ceramics are not popular and the same plate with an unsigned landscape would fetch £40 — £60.

£15 — £20

Josiah Wedgwood 1861
Height 14¾ins:37.4cm. Impressed name and date code

A large, rare and desirable pair of vases by Emile Lessore painted in an unusually clear palette, but in his usual sombre tones, most of his work resembling an oil painting technique.

£1,000 — £1,500

Josiah Wedgwood 1862
Height 7¾ins:19.5cm. Impressed name and date code
A pair of yellow ground earthenware vases painted with
country scenes by Emile Lessore, signed. Lessore was a
pupil of Ingres and came to England in 1858 where he
worked first for Minton and then for Wedgwood for
five years. His work has a strong following.
£700 — £900

Josiah Wedgwood 1865
Height 7½ins:19cm. Impressed name and date code
An earthenware pot-pourri and lozenge-pierced cover
supported on sphinx feet and based on the design of a
tea urn of the early 1880s. The whole under a deep blue,
green and aubergine glaze.
£50 — £70

Josiah Wedgwood 1866
Height 16ins:40.6cm. Impressed name and date code
A large centrepiece in majolica glazes, the detachable
nautilus shell with turquoise interior on the the tails of
green and grey dolphins. Large pieces of marked
Wedgwood majolica have risen considerably over the
last few years. Pair, £400 — £600.
£150 — £200

Josiah Wedgwood 1867
Height 11⅛ins:28.2cm
Impressed name and printed registration of design

A very rare piece of earthenware with a design after Dr. Christopher Dresser symbolising Power. The body a biscuit colour with brown and orange transfer. Exceptionally unusual pieces such as this raise several points regarding the habits of collectors. Too far from the well trodden paths of jasper or basalt and much rarer than any piece of Lessore, despite the registration suggesting that it was made in large numbers, it nevertheless does not command a high price. The collector of the history of design, who is beginning to make his presence felt in the market, usually confines himself in the ceramic field to the Studio market, buying Dresser designs for Linthorpe. He would not be as enthusiastic here as he might be because Dresser has adapted an originally flat pattern on to a new shape, even though this has been done very satisfactorily. The design mark indicates that this was to be a production model and not just a test piece.

£250 — £350

Josiah Wedgwood 1867
Impressed name, Pearl and date code

A dish and sauce tureen from an earthenware service, each piece moulded as a shell, originally produced c.1800. This late example tureen and stand, £60 — £80; sauce tureen, cover and stand, £80 — £120; dishes, £30 — £40; plates, £10 — £15. Compare with the example on p.212.

Josiah Wedgwood 1869
Height 8½ins:21.6cm
Impressed Wedgwood and date code

A majolica tazza of a river putto supporting the disc plate. Well coloured in green, brown, ochre and blue. Pair, £200 — £220.

£80 — £120

Josiah Wedgwood 1870
Impressed Wedgwood and date code

A plate and tazza from a majolica dessert service. The pierced border with key fret, all under a mottled green, brown and yellow "tortoise-shell" glaze. An attractively simple pattern although purists might complain about the clash of cultures evidenced by the rococo dolphins stem and the Chinese key fret.

£200 — £250 (service)

Josiah Wedgwood c.1870
Length 12ins:30.5cm. Impressed name

A rare inkstand dish brightly coloured in the majolica palette with Egyptianesque aspirations, an amusing object of appeal to both Wedgwood and majolica enthusiasts and originally produced in jasper in the late 18th century. Complete with missing central cover, £400 — £500.

£350 — £450

Josiah Wedgwood 1871
Height 5¼ins:13.3cm
Impressed name and registration of design
A good earthenware tea pot naturalistically moulded and coloured as bamboo. Although based on a Chinese original of the 18th century, its production was no doubt sparked off by the fashion for the Japanese in the 1870s. It would look most happy in a Regency setting.
£80 — £100

Josiah Wedgwood 1872
Height 8½ins:21.6cm
Impressed Wedgwood and date code
A scallop shell dish from a service, glazed with mottled greens, browns and yellows. The matching tazze on three dolphin feet. Service of twelve plates, one large and two small tazze, £150 — £200.
£5 — £10

Josiah Wedgwood 1872
Height 10½ins:26.7cm
Impressed name and date code
A majolica figure, probably for use as a flower vase, the basket being hollow. This example with restored hands, in good condition, £200 — £300. With male companion, £500 — £600.
£150 — £200

Josiah Wedgwood 1873
Diameter 9ins:22.9cm. Impressed name, date code
An unusual "Japonaise" earthenware plate transfer printed in black and hand coloured with a scene from Hiroshige's woodblock views of Tokaido with figures and plants. An uncommon pattern. Set of twelve plates, and six tazze in two sizes, £250 — £350.
£10 — £15

Josiah Wedgwood c.1875
Width 10½ins:26.7cm. Impressed Wedgwood
The same dish as that on p.206, but in earthenware and made considerably more interesting by the addition of colourful majolica glazes.
£80 — £120

Josiah Wedgwood 1873
Height 18¾ins:47.6cm
Impressed name and code
A rare creamware vase and cover painted with orchids, the handle and Pegasus knop bronzed and gilded. Despite the quality, rarity and the Wedgwood name, not an expensive object as it falls outside the interest of most Wedgwood collectors. Pair, £250 — £350.
£120 — £140

Josiah Wedgwood 1874
Width 12½ins:31.8cm
Impressed name, registration of design and date code
An attractive majolica dish mottled blue, brown and yellow, the crabstock handle with vine trail. Only over the last two years have these simple dishes shown any great increase in price, and they will probably rise faster than many other categories. A similar piece, lacking marks, £35 — £45.
£50 — £70

Josiah Wedgwood c.1877
Height 6ins:15.2cm. Impressed name and date code
An earthenware tea pot transfer printed in blue with epigrams and figures, possibly adapted from a tile after a design by Thomas Allen. A typical 1870s Japonaiserie shape, spoiled by inappropriate decoration. A part service of tea pot, milk jug and sucrier, £50 — £70.
£15 — £20

Josiah Wedgwood 1877
Diameter 9½ins:24.1cm. Impressed mark and date code

A tazza from an earthenware dessert service printed in brown and hand painted in sombre enamels with a sporting subject. Not common, but not particularly desirable either. Curiously, perhaps, it would fetch more without the printed decoration but with a mottled green-brown glaze, £25 — £35. Plate as shown same price. Service of twelve plates and four tazze each with a different print, £250 — £350.

£25 — £35

Josiah Wedgwood 1878
Diameter 9ins:22.9cm. Impressed name and date code

A thinly potted earthenware plate, attractively printed in brown and hand coloured on the cream body. Service of twelve each soup, dinner and dessert plates, eight meat dishes, soup tureen, cover and stand, sauce tureen, cover and stand and two vegetable dishes and covers, £500 — £600.

Josiah Wedgwood 1877
Width 8ins:20.3cm. Impressed name and date code

An unusual dessert plate transfer printed and hand coloured with miniature Pierrots playing with a soda siphon within a moulded border. Service of twelve plates and three tazze, £180 — £220.

£10 — £15

£8 — £10

214

Josiah Wedgwood c.1879
Height 6½ins:16.3cm
Impressed name, painted pattern number
and moulded registration of design mark

A poorly produced jug, the body indistinctly moulded and coloured with the "Sparrow and Bamboo" pattern. It is a fairly early product of the Aesthetic Movement and has the advantage of being comparable to a plate with a matching design illustrated in the definitive book on the subject, *The Aesthetic Movement* (see Bibliography). The date has been interpreted from the blurred registration mark. Good example, £100 — £150.
£60 — £80

Josiah Wedgwood c.1891
Height 37ins:94cm. Impressed name and date code

A large earthenware jardinière and stand of somewhat heavy proportions in Adam style, palely glazed. The reliefs crisply moulded but with a lack of sensitivity for the original. Odd bowl or column, £50 — £70.
£250 — £300

Josiah Wedgwood last quarter of the 19th century
Diameter 12ins:30.5cm. Impressed name

A large and decorative dish, probably decorated by a visiting artist, a factory artist in his own time or more likely by an amateur at an evening class on a factory blank. This was a common practice at the end of the century and as the supply was completely fortuitous there is no good reason why a Wedgwood marked example should fetch more than say, a Minton piece, but it does. Nevertheless the prices are unpredictable.
£40 — £100

Josiah Wedgwood 1893
9¾ins:25cm. Impressed name and date code

A rare earthenware bowl, or more accurately, rare as it appears here. The piece is a standard line but the decoration is by Bernard Moore in ruby lustre on a grey ground. Moore was a chemist-potter, whose production of a rich ruby lustre was his strongest point, and who used blanks from other factories on which to work. It is not known whether he had any arrangement with Wedgwood but pieces by him on their blanks fetch more than on those of other factories. Ordinary bowl, £60 — £80; with servers, £120 — £180.

£120 — £150

Josiah Wedgwood 1894
19½ins. x 31¼ins:49.5cm x 79.5cm. No mark

A very large earthenware plaque painted by Thomas Allen, signed and dated 1894, in pale enamels. Allen worked for Mintons first and joined Wedgwood in 1875. Had the plaque been marked, the price could be doubled.

£200 — £300

Josiah Wedgwood c.1895
Height 13ins:33cm. Impressed and printed marks
A pair of peach-coloured earthenware vases, palely enamelled and gilded, with peony on a sprayed gilt ground. Of little merit they seem to be copying (unsuccessfully), as do the Fielding vases on p.199, the Royal Worcester porcelain of the period.

£140 — £160

Josiah Wedgwood late 19th century
Height 10ins:25.4cm. Impressed Wedgwood
A rare pair of *rosso antico* candlesticks, the dolphins' tails forming the candle sconces, the black basalt bases with red scallops. Entirely black basalt pair, £1,000 — £1,500; less well modelled, from £500.
£1,800 — £2,000

Josiah Wedgwood 1900
9½ins:24cm. Impressed name and date code
A creamware basket based on an 18th century original
but without the quality. Without the mark, £15 — £20.
£50 — £70

Josiah Wedgwood c.1910
Height 14ins:36.7cm. Impressed Wedgwood
An earthenware vase painted in blue and brown slips
with a Chinese lotus design on a buff ground. A strong
attribution can be made to the hand of Harry Barnard
who decorated from the turn of the century until 1930.
£80 — £120

Josiah Wedgwood 1913
13½ins:43.3cm
Impressed mark and code and printed mark
A rare and early butterfly lustre bowl and the only piece
to have come to notice on an earthenware body, the
decoration in bright enamels and gilding. As it is
normally impossible to date these lustres, this example is
particularly interesting.
£300 — £400

Josiah Wedgwood c.1930
Height 7ins:17.7cm. Impressed names
An art deco doe after an original by John Skeaping and one of a set of twelve, his name moulded into the base, the whole under a green glaze. These 'thirties models are just beginning to be appreciated.

£100 — £120

Josiah Wedgwood 1928
Height 7ins:18cm. Impressed name
A curiosity from the factory painted in green, blue and silver lustre by Cecily Stella Wedgwood on a body thrown by Clement Tom Wedgwood. The factory seemed to suffer from a surfeit of visiting artists and others who tried their hand, usually at decoration and usually unsuccessfully.

£60 — £80

Josiah Wedgwood 1937
Width 5¼ins:13.3cm
Impressed name and printed inscription
A glazed box and cover applied with a blue portrait of Edward VIII and the date 1937 to commemorate the forthcoming Coronation. Definitely not of interest to Wedgwood collectors but likely to appeal more to the commemorative market.

£15 — £20

Wedgwood: Jasper and Basalt

**Wedgwood and
Bentley/Wedgwood
18th and early 19th century
8¾ins:22.2cm
Impressed Wedgwood
and Bentley**

An interesting object lesson for the
unwary. A pair of mottled manganese
and green earthenware vases from the
early years of the 19th century,
mounted on to perfectly genuine
earlier bases made about 1775. They
may well be unmarried by the dealer
who buys them to supply right bases
for a right pair missing them. Vases
alone, £80 — £120.
£200 — £300

**Josiah Wedgwood c.1810
10ins:25.4cm. Impressed Wedgwood**

A black basalt coffee pot painted in brilliant
famille rose enamels with chrysanthemums over a
black print outline.
£80 — £150

**Josiah Wedgwood c.1830
4½ins:11.4cm. Impressed name**

A rare black basalt tobacco jar and cover
sparsely decorated in *famille rose* enamels. The
interior has a flat weight to press the tobacco.
Lacking weight, £60 — £80.
£100 — £150

Josiah Wedgwood c.1840
9½ins:24.1cm. Impressed name

A good black basalt pot-pourri, lid and cover brightly painted in *famille rose* enamels with peony and prunus. The lack of the inner lid would make about a 5% difference to the price.

£320 — £400

Josiah Wedgwood c.1845
6½ins:16.5cm. Impressed Wedgwood

A three colour jasper tea pot and stand, the rather muddy white body with green and pale brown reliefs. Clean example, £200 — £300.

£150 — £200

Josiah Wedgwood mid-19th century
21¾ins:55.2cm. Impressed name and title

A good black basalt figure of Eros and Euphrosyne, well cast in a rich black body and with a polished patina.

£400 — £500

Josiah Wedgwood mid-19th century
22ins:56cm. Impressed name

A black basalt faun and goat and so titled from impressed type on the base. Not as well produced as the previous example, as the mould marks are very prominent.

£300 — £400

Josiah Wedgwood mid-19th century
14ins:35.6cm. Impressed name
A black basalt dip pot-pourri vase and cover with its
infitting lid. Pair, £500 — £700.
£250 — £350

Josiah Wedgwood mid-19th century
13¼ins:33.5cm. Impressed name
A black basalt bust of the poet Thomas Moore, the
name impressed on the back. Typical of the classical
treatment of poets and authors, the prices vary little.
The example well cast and with a fine polished patina.
£300 — £400

Josiah Wedgwood mid-19th century
7¾ins:19.7cm. Impressed name
A blue jasper dip vase of good quality and attractively
simple design. Pair, £120 — £150.
£30 — £50

Josiah Wedgwood mid-19th century
13½ins:34.3cm. Impressed Wedgwood
A blue jasper dip vase with the Apotheosis of Homer
after John Flaxman. A rare design which originally
appeared with a cover. Complete, £500 — £800.
£250 — £350

**Josiah Wedgwood
Mid-19th century
3½ins:9cm. Impressed name**
An unusual three colour scent bottle with lilac-ground panels on a blue body. The mount in this case in gilt metal. Similar in silver-gilt, £280 — £320.
£280 — £300

**Josiah Wedgwood
Mid-19th century
8½ins:21.6cm. Impressed name**
A well executed vase and cover in black jasper dip, the reliefs crisp and clean but the design somewhat overcrowded. Pair, £600 — £900.
£200 — £300

**Josiah Wedgwood
Mid-19th century
9¼ins:23.5cm. Impressed name**
A canopic urn and cover in black basalt, crisply moulded after a burial urn used in Ancient Egypt. A good quality example with a fine polished sheen to the body. The blackness of the material used can vary quite considerably in all basalt wares, the more dense the better.
£800 — £1,000

**Josiah Wedgwood 1877
9¾ins:24.7cm
Impressed name and date code**
A variation on the last example, the green dipped body with white reliefs. Large pieces of this sort rarely bear date codes. A blue jasper dip example would fetch £650 — £800.
£700 — £900

223

THE SENTRY BOX

Josiah Wedgwood
Second half of the 19th century
5¼ins:13.3cm. Impressed name
A blue jasper dip oil lamp, the reliefs of two maidens
and Cupid surrounded by signs of the Zodiac. Well
executed and attractive in form, it makes an ideal
cabinet object.

£180 — £200

Josiah Wedgwood
Second half of the 19th century
5ins:12.9cm. Impressed name
A crisply moulded relief in white on pale blue after a
relief by A.B. Wyon from the painting by C.R. Leslie of
Uncle Toby, a character in Lawrence Sterne's novel
Tristam Shandy. The subject also appears on a pot-lid.
£140 — £180

Josiah Wedgwood
Second half of the 19th century
3⅝ins:9.2cm. Impressed name
A tea pot with olive green jasper dip ground crudely applied
with classical figures. Originally part of a tête-à-tête: tea pot,
milk jug, sucrier, basin and two cups and saucers, £120 —
£150.

£30 — £50

Josiah Wedgwood
Second half of the 19th century
9½ins:24.1cm. Impressed name
A blue jasper dip urn and cover moulded with white figures.
Of reasonable quality, the mouldings sharp but cracked in the
firing and the mould mark on the handle on the left is clear in
the photograph; always a pointer to an item not having had as
much care taken over it as it might.

	Pairs
Blue ground £100 — £150	*Blue £250 — £350*
Black ground £120 — £180	*Black £330 — £500*
Sage ground £100 — £150	*Sage £350 — £500*

Josiah Wedgwood 1870
Diameter of saucer 5½ins:14cm
Impressed name and date code

A three colour jasper coffee can and saucer, the cane coloured body with sage green borders and lilac medallions applied with white reliefs. The three colours play a large part in dictating the price, the comparable two colour piece would be in the region of £60 — £80. The colour of the ground also plays a part and so does the clarity of that colour as cane wares are particularly prone to discolouration as in this example; a really fine specimen, £300 — £350.

£250 — £350

Josiah Wedgwood late 19th century
Diameter of saucer 5¼ins:13.4cm. Impressed name

Another three colour piece of high quality but less unusual than the last, the reliefs being in lilac and white on the pale blue ground. The similar price achieved by the good condition.

£250 — £350

Josiah Wedgwood c.1880
Height 12¾ins:32.4cm. Impressed Wedgwood

A vast blue jasper dip tobacco jar and cover made for a club or shop. This example with a known pedigree from the latter. Although uncommon, its large size prevents it selling well, as with almost all Wedgwood.

£120 — £200

225

Josiah Wedgwood probably 1887
Height 6½ins:16.5cm
Impressed name and blurred code
A blue jasper cache-pot applied with swags and panels. Cache-pots and jardinières tend not to fetch as much as one might expect, possibly because their obviously utilitarian use makes them awkward to display.

£140 — £180

Josiah Wedgwood late 19th century
7½ins:19.1cm. Impressed Wedgwood
A pair of green jasper dip pot-pourri, the pierced lids invisible inside. The harebells are a frequently seen motif but the overall appearance is unexciting.

£200 — £250

Josiah Wedgwood late 19th century
7¾ins:19.7cm. Impressed Wedgwood
A small black basalt vase with poorly moulded borders and figures. Singles of this size are unpopular unless particularly rare. Pair, £60 — £80.

£18 — £20

Josiah Wedgwood late 19th century
6ins. x 17¾ins:15cm x 45cm. Impressed name and England
A black basalt dip plaque that appears quite frequently but being of large size and decorative it is much in demand.
The white relief is of Hercules accepting Virtue pointing upwards to the heavenly temple, while Pleasure lies rejected
on a couch, a nymph and satyr dancing behind in a grove.
£400 — £600

Josiah Wedgwood late 19th century
7¼ins:18.4cm. Impressed name
A rare three colour plate, the central panel in lilac and
with white reliefs on a blue ground. Plates are
uncommon.

£450 — £550

Josiah Wedgwood late 19th century
6¼ins. x 8¾ins:16cm x 22cm. Impressed name
A pair of black basalt dip plaques of putti at a wedding
or making a sacrifice.

£280 — £320

Josiah Wedgwood late 19th century
Height 17ins:43.2cm. Impressed Wedgwood
A pair of black basalt wine and water ewers after designs by John Flaxman, one with Neptune at the neck, the other Bacchus. They seem to have been made from the 18th century until the present day, generally to a high standard. Single, £250 — £350.
£600 — £800

Josiah Wedgwood late 19th century
Height 8ins:20.3cm
Impressed Wedgwood
An uncommon clockcase in blue jasper dip applied in white. Clockcases seem under-priced particularly when of unusual form or decoration.
£120 — £180

Josiah Wedgwood
Early 20th century
Height 15ins:38.1cm
Impressed name
A not very good refinement on the above examples with the addition of gilding. Rare and therefore desirable but spoiling the whole essence of Flaxman's brilliant design which depends on the simplicity of the plain black body. Pair, £800 — £1,000.
£300 — £350

Josiah Wedgwood late 19th century
3⅝ins:9.2cm. Impressed name
A small blue jasper dip box and cover with a sacrificial altar. The same in carmine dip, £200 — £250.
£50 — £80

228

Josiah Wedgwood c.1900
Height 10ins:25.4cm
Impressed name and England
Two blue jasper plaques with white classical figures of a type that appears frequently although usually of smaller size. They were made for setting in mounts on furniture but could be put to other uses; these were removed from a ceiling frieze in a London house. Years of neglect and cigarette smoke, which only strong bleach might remove, have discoloured them.
£60 — £80 each

Josiah Wedgwood
c.1900
Height 12¼ins:31.2cm
Impressed name
A black basalt figure of Innocence, the title impressed in the base. The mould mark at the junction of the shoulder can be clearly seen and the black is not of the intensity that it should be. Better examples, £300 — £400.
£250 — £350

Josiah Wedgwood c.1900
Height 10ins:25.5cm. Impressed name
Another oval plaque but a better subject than the previous examples helped by the sharp leaf border and the sage ground. Pair, £300 — £400.
£120 — £180

Josiah Wedgwood c.1900
Width 2½ins:6.5cm
Incised title, impressed Wedgwood
A blue jasper plaque with the white relief portrait of
George III under a crown and the words "Health
Restored", referring to his apparent return to sanity in
1789. Like most 18th century portrait plaques they
continued in production throughout the 19th and into
the 20th century. Large numbers of different portraits
exist but the copies all tend to fetch about £50 — £80;
black basalt is at a slight premium and attractive mounts
will affect the price, as in this example.
£60 — £80

Josiah Wedgwood c.1900
Height 7⅛ins:18cm. Impressed name
A pair of blue jasper dip candlesticks applied with
classical figures. Candlesticks are not common but not
much in demand either.
£70 — £90

Josiah Wedgwood early 20th century
Height 3ins:7.6cm. Impressed name and England
A crimson dip match pot and cover applied with white
reliefs. Crimson is a rare ground colour, possibly
because it seems to have suffered from technical
difficulties — it is usually uneven and the white reliefs,
as in this example, discoloured. A good example would
fetch 50% — 80% more.
£180 — £250

Josiah Wedgwood early 20th century
Width 4¼ins:10.8cm. Impressed Wedgwood, England
A crimson ground box and cover of poor quality, the
applied decoration badly cast and cracked in the firing.
Good example, £180 — £250.
£140 — £160

**Josiah Wedgwood
Early 20th century
Height 8¼ins:22.3cm
Impressed name
and Made in England**

A pair of black basalt busts of Sir Walter Scott and Lord Byron. The material not a dense black and the moulding not as crisp as it should be, the mould marks are visible on the necks and faces. These minus points combined with the smaller size make them considerably less expensive than the earlier bust of Moore on p.222.

£350 — £450

**Josiah Wedgwood early 20th century
Height 5¾ins:14.7cm. Impressed Wedgwood, England**

Another crimson ground piece, sucrier and cover, but again the production is not up to the usual Wedgwood standard although this is better than most crimson grounds. Better example, £220 — £250.

£180 — £220

**Josiah Wedgwood
Early 20th century
6¾ins:17.2cm**

Impressed Wedgwood, Made in England

A biscuit barrel with an unusual mustard-yellow jasper dip ground applied with black figures. The mount and cover as usual electro-plated.

£160 — £180

231

The Portland Vase

Figure I

Figure II

The famous Graeco-Roman cameo glass vase, known as the Barbarini or Portland, was lent by the Duke of Portland, and copied by Josiah Wedgwood in 1790 in an edition of no more than ten, some of which did not appear until the early years of the nineteenth century. All were of very fine translucency; the white was sharpened on the lapidiary's wheel over a dense blue background. These are usually numbered in pencil inside the rim and are unmarked. Examples were sold in 1974 and 1975 for between £18,000 and £20,000.

The vase was loaned to the British Museum, where it still is, and was smashed by a lunatic in 1845. Wedgwood's have issued numerous variations with varying degrees of success.

The earliest nineteenth century examples were again straight copies as in the black basalt example Figure I, and the blue jasper reverse Figure II, but prudery dictated the introduction of strategic drapery in 1839, Figure III. The Phrygian head, Figure V, on the base may, or may not, be present; the size can range from six to eleven inches; the quality varies. These factors taken together with the possibility of colour variation (solid black basalt, black basalt dip or jasper and jasper dip in the usual blue or in sage green or yellow) means a price range from £30 — £1,000. Additionally, John Northwood, the glass engraver, who was first to copy the vase in glass in 1875, and which was sold at Sotheby's Belgravia in 1976 for £30,000, despite having been broken into several pieces by the artist, sharpened about ten Wedgwood copies on his engraver's wheel, marking them with his initials. One of these would fetch about £4,000 — £8,000. The Wedgwood potter, Thomas Lovatt, marked some of the vases he worked on with his impressed name and these fetch about £800 — £1,200. The table opposite is a guide to the prices but quality is all important here.

The last issue was between 1971 and 1979 in blue and white, ten inches, in an edition of fifty at £1,490 each.

All nineteenth century jasper and basalt is difficult to date, particularly as Wedgwood seems to have ignored the McKinley Tariff Acts of 1891 and 1902.

Figure III

Figure V

PRICES FOR THE PORTLAND VASE

Height in Inches	Black Basalt	Blue Jasper or Dip
6ins.	£120 — £200	£100 — £150
8ins.	£250 — £400	£180 — £220
10 + ins.	£400 — £600	£350 — £500

ADDED DRAPERY

6ins.	£100 — £150	£80 — £150
8ins.	£180 — £250	£150 — £200
10 + ins.	£350 — £500	£300 — £350

Without head on base 10-20% LESS
For other colours 20-30% MORE

Figure IV

**Josiah Wedgwood
Mid-19th century
10¼ins:26cm
Impressed Wedgwood**
A rare variation on the usual jasper with the white body showing the reliefs against an applied dark shiny blue background. The result is decidedly unsatisfactory.
£320 — £350

Appendix I
Fakes

The collector of nineteenth century British pottery is still quite secure when it comes to fakes. There has been little, up until the last few years, to warrant the serious attention of the faker with the exception of the continuation of the production of a few Staffordshire models, particularly dogs, mostly from the original moulds. With some figures now in the upper hundreds for an object which is cheap to produce from easily obtained clay and glazes and fired at a low temperature, it is inevitable that more and more dubious figures will come on the market. The boxers (figure 1) are a fair example of a recast from the original Heenan and Sayers, p.159. They display many of the faults found with copies, such as the too smooth and black hair and boots, and poorly drawn features, the ill considered gilding and the flat pink of the bodies. These superficial characteristics are, however, nothing like as condemning as the inherent faults in the production such as the difference in size caused by the shrinkage in the clay during the firing process, in this case from the original 13ins. to 8⅜ins. (22cm). The Price Guide can be used to establish the size of the original figures,

Figure 2

anything smaller should be looked at with care, but remember that many figures were made in different sizes. If in doubt check with P.D. Gordon-Pugh (see Bibliography). Perhaps the best guide to modern reproductions is the glaze crackle, wrong in figure 2 and right in figure 3. In the former the glaze is tight to the body and, where it forms pools, is glassy and clear and the crazing very uniform and the cracks brown. On the original the glaze varies in thickness, often forming blobs at the base and pools where it is a distinctly blue colour, the crazing being clear or black.

The Staffordshire cottage (figure 4) is a far more sophisticated fake than Heenan and Sayers; the glaze is only slightly too shiny and with a far more convincing crackle, but the base has the same wiped-clean look as the former. The colours do not have the same density of shade as the originals and they are too heavily potted. These houses are appearing with different names and places in country sales rooms. Compare with the original on p.89.

Another form of fake which appears fairly regularly is the spirit flask or jug, reproducing in earthenware what should be stoneware. The jug in figure 5 apparently commemorates the death of Wellington in 1852 but the lettering is the best give-away of the reproduction. On the originals it was impressed from bookbinders' or printers' type and is crisp and clear, on the copies it forms part of the mould and the definition is lost. Here the jug is under a brown glaze that is far too shiny and consistent. The spirit flask in figure 6 is under a more mottled glaze on a greyish body, both have the curious thinning of the glaze round the bottom of the piece. Compare with an original on p.34.

I have recently seen, and they are apparently turning up in country salerooms in fair numbers, porcelain jugs and vases with black photo-lithographic copies of the Victoria and other coronation prints. It is hard to

Figure 1

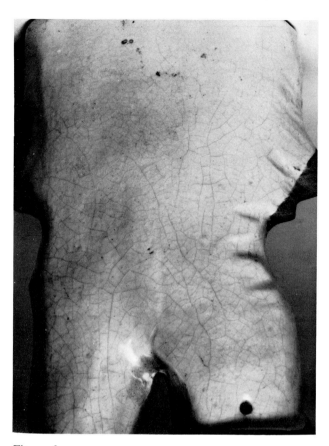

Figure 3

Figure 5

Figure 4

Figure 6

235

Figure 8

Figure 7

believe that they would fool anyone with any knowledge, but the marks on the piece I saw had been ground off the base, and an attempt is being made at deception.

Figure 7 illustrates an awful warning to the unwary, the dish appearing as a perfectly respectable piece of George Jones majolica moulded with leaves, cherries and twigs under the usual bright, clear glazes. The close up detail in figure 8 just discloses the deception; the squirrel which originally sat on the twigs has been broken off and the remains ground down leaving only traces of the feet, the stumps having been restored. A complete nut dish is illustrated on p.128.

Sunderland lustre is a great problem as the jugs and mugs with famous bridges have been in almost continuous production since 1800 and it is impossible to decide whether one made in 1820, 1850, 1900, 1930 or a brand new one is a fake. The earlier the piece, generally speaking, the finer and lighter the body and the better the pink splashing.

For those interested the following prices are given as a guide of what one might have to pay for them *as fakes*. Figure 1, £10 — £15; figure 4, £15 — £20; figure 5, £10 — £15; figure 6, £8 — £12; figure 7, 50p — £2.

Appendix II
Factories

Samuel Alcock & Co., Cobridge, c.1828-53.

G.L. Ashworth & Brothers, Hanley, Staffordshire, 1862 to present day.

Booths, Tunstall, Staffordshire, 1891-1948.

William Brownfield, Cobridge, Staffordshire, 1850-91.

Burmantofts, Leeds, Yorkshire, 1882-1904.

Samuel and John Burton, Hanley, 1832-45.

Carlton Ware see Wiltshaw and Robinson.

Castleford, see David Dunderdale & Co.

James and Ralph Clews, Cobridge, Staffordshire, 1818-34.

Clyde Pottery Co., Greenock, Scotland, 1815-1903.

Copeland and Garrett, Stoke-on-Trent, Staffordshire, 1833-47.

W.T. Copeland, Spode Works, Stoke-on-Trent, 1847 to present day.

Davenport, Longport, 1793-1887.

Deakin and Son, Waterloo Works, Lane End, Staffordshire, 1833-41.

Dillwyn, see Swansea Pottery.

Dixon, Austin and Co., Sunderland, Durham, c.1820-26.

Dixon Phillips and Co., Sunderland Pottery, Durham, 1840-65.

Don Pottery, Swinton, Yorkshire, 1790-1893.

Doulton and Co., Lambeth, c.1858-1956, and Nile Street, Burslem, 1882 to present day (Royal after 1902).

Doulton & Watts, Lambeth, c.1815-58.

David Dunderdale & Co., Castleford Pottery, Yorkshire, c.1790-1820.

Elkin, Knight and Bridgewood, Fenton, Staffordshire, 1827-40.

Thomas Fell and Co., Newcastle-upon-Tyne, Northumberland, 1817-90.

A. Fenton & Sons, Hanley, Staffordshire, 1887-1901.

S. Fielding & Co., Stoke-on-Trent, 1879 to present day.

J. & R. Godwin, Cobridge, Staffordshire, 1834-66.

Goodwin, Bridgewood and Harris, Lane End, Staffordshire, 1829-31.

Stephen Green, Lambeth, c.1828-58.

Hackwood, several potters of this name, Shelton and Hanley, c.1800-c.1860.

William Hackwood, Hanley, Staffordshire, 1827-43.

James Hadley and Sons, Worcester, 1896-1905.

John Hall, Burslem, 1814-32.

Joshua Heath, Hanley, Staffordshire, 1770-1810?

Herculaneum Pottery, Liverpool, 1793-1841.

Robert Heron (Wemyss), Kirkaldy, 1850-1929.

Hicks and Meigh, Shelton, Staffordshire, 1806-22.

Hill Pottery Co. see Samuel Alcock & Co.

Johnson Brothers, Hanley, Staffordshire, 1883 to present day.

George Jones, Trent Pottery, Stoke-on-Trent, 1864-1907.

Langley, see Lovatt & Lovatt.

Leeds Pottery, Hunslet, Leeds, Yorkshire, c.1758-1820.

John Lloyd, Shelton, Hanley, Staffordshire, c.1834-52.

Lovatt & Lovatt, Langley Mill, Nr. Nottingham, 1895 to present day.

G.M. & C.J. Mason, Lane Delph, Staffordshire, 1813-29.

Charles James Mason & Co., 1829-45.

Charles James Mason, Fenton Works, Lane Delph, Staffordshire, 1843-48 and Longton 1851-54.

Charles Meigh, Hanley, Staffordshire, 1835-49.

Charles Meigh & Sons, Hanley, 1851-61.

David Methven and Sons, Kirkcaldy, Fifeshire, first half 19th century to c.1930.

Minton, Stoke-on-Trent, Staffordshire, 1793 to present day (Mintons after 1873).

Moore and Co., Wear Pottery, Southwick, Sunderland, 1803-74.

Francis Morley, Hanley, Staffordshire, 1845-58.

Newport Pottery Co. Ltd., Burslem, Staffordshire, 1920 to present day.

Edward and George Phillips, Longport, Staffordshire, 1822-34.

Pinder, Bourne & Co., Burslem, 1862-82.

Felix Pratt, Fenton, Staffordshire.

F. & R. Pratt and Co., Fenton, Staffordshire, 1818-1920.

W. Ridgway, Son and Co., Hanley, Staffordshire, 1838-48.

Robinson and Leadbeater, Stoke-on-Trent, 1864-1924.

John Rogers and Son, Longport, Staffordshire, 1814-36.

James Sadler and Sons, Burslem, Staffordshire, 1899 to present day.

St. Anthony's Pottery, Newcastle-upon-Tyne, Northumberland, 1780-1820.

Obadiah Sherrat.

Sherwin and Cotton, Vine Street, Hanley, Staffordshire, 1877-1930.

Shorthose and Co., Hanley, Staffordshire, c.1817-22.

William Smith and Co., Stock-on-Tees, Durham, c.1845-84.

Josiah Spode, Stoke-on-Trent, Staffordshire, c.1774-1833; (Spode and Copeland 1797-1816).

Andrew Stevenson, Cobridge, Staffordshire, c.1816-30.

Ralph Stevenson and Williams, Cobridge, Staffordshire, c.1825.

Swansea Pottery, Wales, c.1783-1870.

John Walton, Burslem, Staffordshire, c.1818-35.

Watcombe Pottery Co., St. Mary Church, Devon, 1867-1901.

Josiah Wedgwood, various addresses, 1759 to present day.

Wemyss see Robert Heron.

Wiltshaw and Robinson, Stoke-on-Trent, Staffordshire, 1890 to present day.

Wood and Caldwell, Burslem, 1790-1818.

Enoch Wood and Sons, Burslem, Staffordshire, 1818-46.

Royal Worcester Porcelain Company Ltd., Worcester, 1862 to present day.

Appendix III
Calendar of
People and Events

1800   George III on throne; parliamentary Union of Great Britain and Ireland.

1804   Napoleon Bonaparte becomes Emperor.

1805   Battle of Trafalgar, Nelson killed.

1807   Slave Trade abolished in Britain.

1808   Peninsular War begins.

1809/1810   George III Golden Jubilee.

1812   Napoleon's retreat from Moscow.

1813   Wellington defeats French at Victoria.

1814   Napoleon abdicates.

1815   Napoleon escapes from Elba; Battle of Waterloo; Corn Law passed.

1817   Princess Charlotte (daughter of Prince Regent, later George IV) dies.

1820   George III dies, George IV succeeds; Queen Caroline returns from Italy.

1821   Napoleon dies at St. Helena; Queen Caroline (abused wife of George IV) dies.

1824   Trades Unions become legal.

1825   Stockton and Darlington Railway opened.

1829   Roman Catholic Emancipation Act passed.

1830   George IV dies, William IV succeeds.

1831   William and Adelaide crowned.

1832   Reform Bill passed.

1834   Tolpuddle Martys.

1836   Chartists' movement.

1837   William IV dies, Victoria succeeds.

1838   Victoria crowned.

1840   Victoria marries Prince Albert of Saxe-Coberg-Gotha.

1846   Repeal of Corn Laws led by Sir Robert Peel.

1848   Louis Phillippe of France abdicates, French Republic proclaimed.

1850   Sir Robert Peel dies.

1851   Great Exhibition (Crystal Palace).

1852   Napoleon III becomes Emperor of France; Arthur Wellesley, Duke of Wellington, dies.

1853   Russia and Turkey at war.

1854   France and Britain declare war on Russia, troops landed in Crimea, battles of Alma, Balaclava, Inkerman, and siege of Sebastopol.

1855   Sardinia joins allies, Sebastopol falls, war ends.

1856   Peace Treaty signed in Paris.

1857   Indian Mutiny, Lucknow relieved.

1858   John Brown hanged; Princess Royal marries Prince Frederick William of Prussia.

1861   American Civil War starts; Victor Emanuel proclaimed King of Italy; Prince Albert dies.

1862   Garibaldi wounded attempting to seize Rome; International Exhibition in London.

1863   Prince of Wales marries Princess Alexandra of Denmark.

1865   Lincoln assassinated; slavery abolished in U.S; Palmerston dies.

1866 Austro-Prussian War.
1870 Napoleon III declares war against Prussia and is defeated; Siege of Paris; Irish Land Act passed.
1871 Paris falls.
1874 Disraeli succeeds Gladstone as Prime Minister.
1877 Victoria Empress of India; Transvaal becomes British.
1879 France and Britain control Egypt.
1881 Transvaal independant.
1882 Cairo occupied by British troops.
1884 Gordon trapped in Khartoum.
1885 Gordon killed at Khartoum.
1886 Home Rule Bill defeated in Commons.
1887 Victoria's Golden Jubilee.
1897 Victoria's Diamond Jubilee "Sixty Years A Queen".
1899 Boer War.
1900 Boers lay siege to Kimberley and Ladysmith; Baden Powell defends Mafeking.
1901 Victoria dies, Albert Edward, Edward VII succeeds.
1902 Coronation Edward VII and Alexandra.
1910 Edward VII dies, George V succeeds.
1911 George V crowned.
1914 Start of First World War.
1918 End of First World War.
1936 George V dies, Edward VIII succeeds and abdicates before coronation.
1937 George VI crowned.
1951 Festival of Britain.

Bibliography

E. Aslin, *The Aesthetic Movement,* London, 1969.

P. Atterbury and L. Irvine, *The Doulton Story,* Victoria and Albert Museum, London, 1979.

T. Balston, *Staffordshire Portrait Figures of the Victorian Age,* London, 1958.

J. Barnard, *Victorian Ceramic Tiles,* London, 1972.

D.A. Battie and M. Turner, *The Price Guide to 19th and 20th Century British Porcelain,* Woodbridge, 1975.

R.C. Bell, *Tyneside Pottery,* 1971.

G. Bemrose, *Nineteenth Century English Pottery and Porcelain,* London, 1952.

J.F. Blacker, *19th Century English Ceramic Art,* London, n.d.

A.W. Coysh, *Blue and White Transfer Printed Ware 1780-1840,* Newton Abbot, 1970.

A.W. Coysh, *Blue-printed Earthenware 1800-1850,* Newton Abbot, 1972.

D. Eyles, *The Doulton Lambeth Wares,* London, 1974.

D. Eyles, *Royal Doulton 1815-1965,* London, 1965.

G.A. Godden, *An Illustrated Encyclopaedia,* London, 1966.

G.A. Godden, *British Pottery,* London, 1974.

G.A. Godden, *Encyclopaedia of British Pottery and Porcelain Marks,* London, 1964.

G.A. Godden, *Mason's Patent Ironstone China,* London, 1971.

G.A. Godden, *Minton Pottery and Porcelain of the First Period,* London, 1968.

P.D. Gordon-Pugh, *Staffordshire Portrait Figures,* London, 1970.

J. Jefferson Miller II, *English Yellow-Glazed Earthenware,* London, 1974.

L. Jewitt, *The Ceramic Art of Great Britain, London,* 1972.

A. Kelly, *The Story of Wedgwood,* London, 1975.

E.B. Larsen, *American Historical Views on Staffordshire China,* 3rd ed., New York, 1975.

H. Lawrence, *Yorkshire Pots and Potters,* Newton Abbot, 1974.

W.L. Little, *Staffordshire Blue,* London, 1969.

T.A. Lockett, *Davenport Pottery and Porcelain,* London, 1972.

A. Oliver, *Victorian Staffordshire Figures,* London, 1971.

H. Sandon, *Royal Worcester Porcelain,* London, 1973.

J.T. Shaw, Editor, *Sunderland Ware,* Sunderland Public Libraries, Museum and Art Gallery, revised edition, 1973.

A. Smith, *Liverpool Herculaneum Pottery,* 1970.

L.T. Stanley, *Collecting Staffordshire Pottery,* London, 1963.

H. Wakefield, *Victorian Pottery,* London, 1962.

L. Whiter, *Spode — A History of the Family and Wares,* London, 1970.

Index